GOD, SKY & LAND

"What could be more important in the creation/evolution debate, especially for those who derive their views from Scripture, than to try and hear Genesis 1 as its original hearers heard it?! And who better to help us do that than two of Adventism's most capable scholars and devoted churchmen . . . I heartily recommend their enlightened attempt." —*Lawrence Geraty, former president, American Schools of Oriental Research*

"The obvious research and study give good reason to believe that our Creator meets all of us just where we are, whether hearers or readers." —*Dan Matthews, Speaker Emeritus, Faith for Today Television*

"Rejecting the existence of a disconnect between Genesis and science, Bull and Guy firmly agree with the Genesis author that 'every thing that was, is, or even will be, exists because of God.'" —*William Loveless, former senior pastor, Loma Linda University Church*

". . . a stunning success, forcing us to rethink our assumptions [and] listen with greater sensitivity to what Bible writers originally intended to communicate." —*Douglas R. Clark, professor of Biblical studies and archaeology, La Sierra University*

"Helpful interpretation of Genesis 1 depends on what the authors call 'retro-translation'—translation that allows today's readers to inhabit (if imperfectly) a conceptual world radically different from our own. Bull and Guy provide such a translation and show how it opens doors to a more honest and illuminating account of divine creation. Not that they settle every issue: their book will ignite a thousand conversations." —*Charles Scriven, president, Kettering College, Dayton, Ohio*

Best wishes,
    Fritz Guy
Warm Regards
    Brian Bull

GOD, SKY & LAND

GENESIS 1 *as the* ANCIENT HEBREWS HEARD IT

BRIAN BULL & FRITZ GUY

ADVENTIST FORUM
Roseville, California

ADVENTIST FORUM
P.O. Box 619047
Roseville, CA 95661-9047
www.spectrummagazine.org

Designed and illustrated by Heather Langley
Edited by Tim Lale

2011908904

Printed in the United States of America
1 2 3 4 5 • 15 14 13 12 11

DEDICATED

*to our grandchildren
in the hope that Genesis 1 will bring to their lives
meaning that science is unable to provide*

TABLE OF CONTENTS

THE APPARENT DISCONNECT

GENESIS VERSUS SCIENCE

For almost two thousand years Christians have pored over the biblical texts in an earnest effort to understand them. The greatest minds of the church have spent themselves in this consecrated endeavor. Not least among their concerns has been what the Bible teaches about creation. For this they turned especially to Genesis 1:1–2:3, and studies of the ["six days"] loom large among the writings they have left us.[1]

WE WISH IT were otherwise, but there is no getting around the fact that there is a profound disconnect between science (as commonly understood) and Genesis (as usually read), a disconnect that has existed since the scientific revolution began in the sixteenth century. This book is about Genesis 1—that is, more specifically, about Genesis 1:1–2:4a, which is what we will always mean by "Genesis 1" in this work.

An abundance of evidence—some of which can be seen by

---

1. John H. Stek, "What Says the Scripture?" in *Portraits of Creation: Biblical and Scientific Perspectives on the World's Formation,* ed. Howard J. Van Till et al. (Grand Rapids, MI: Eerdmans, 1990), 205.

nonscientists with their own eyes if they look in the appropriate places—indicates that Earth is very, very old and that life upon it has been changing gradually for a long, long time (maybe billions of years). On the other hand, the Biblical[2] genealogies together with the Creation hymn in Genesis 1 suggest to many readers that Earth is something less than ten thousand years old and that all life forms came into existence in six literal, twenty-four-hour, consecutive, contiguous days during the same week in which Earth itself was created.

The gulf between these two views could hardly be larger, yet many other readers—including Christian laypersons, theologians, and Bible-believing, church-going scientists—are convinced that there must be a way to accept both modern science and Genesis 1. After all, is not one God the ultimate Source of everything that is—including energy, matter, life, consciousness, and spirituality?

For the several hundred years that the apparent disconnect between Genesis and science has persisted, there have been two main camps. Christians of a more conservative outlook have insisted that the controversy will be settled ultimately in favor of a literal understanding of the Genesis account. While science may, for the time being, not be supportive of this view, science often changes its opinions, these Christians say, and it will eventually come around to a short chronology both for Earth and for life upon it.

But many practicing Christians who are also practicing scientists disagree.[3] For more than three hundred years they have watched

---

2. Although it is the usual scholarly practice not to capitalize the word *biblical* (as exemplified in the quotation above from John Stek), we have elected to do so in this book, both because of the more general practice in English to capitalize adjectives derived from proper nouns and because of the tendency to capitalize the word in popular Christian writing.

3. See, for example, the eighteen contributors to *Real Scientists, Real Faith*, ed. R. J. Berry (Grand Rapids, MI: Monarch, 2009). These include Francis Collins, who from 1993 to 2008 was director of the National Genome Project and since 2009 has been director of the National Institutes of Health;

evidence accumulate that the earth is billions of years old, that the universe is even older (by something like nine billion years), and that living things have long inhabited Earth in ever-changing forms. Convinced by the weight of evidence from cosmology and astrophysics, biology and paleontology, geology and geochronology, genetics and genomics, they have concluded that the Genesis story must be figurative and nonliteral—that it must be poetry, metaphor, or myth.

So this seems to be the present situation:

For many Christians: Science is a weak reed, and inspired Scripture is the only reliable authority on the age of the earth and the origin of life upon it.

---

and Simon Conway Morris, professor of evolutionary paleobiology at the University of Cambridge.

Evangelical Christians who espouse an evolutionary understanding of natural history include Karl Giberson, professor of physics at Eastern Nazarene University, who has published *Saving Darwin: How to Be a Christian and Believe in Evolution* (New York: HarperOne, 2008); and Denis O. Lamoureux, associate professor of science and religion at St. Joseph's College, University of Alberta, who has published *Evolutionary Creation: A Christian Approach to Evolution* (Eugene, OR: Wipf and Stock, 2008) and the less formidable *I Love Jesus & I Accept Evolution* (Eugene, OR: Wipf and Stock, 2009). The latter book carries an epigraph by Billy Graham that begins, "I don't think that there's any conflict at all between science today and the Scriptures."

Also to be mentioned here are three contemporary scientist-theologians—Ian G. Barbour, physicist and professor of religion at Carleton College in Minnesota; Arthur Peacocke (1924–2006), biochemist, priest and honorary canon of Christ Church, Oxford; and John Polkinghorne, theoretical physicist, theologian, Anglican priest, and prolific author. For an overview of their similarities and differences, see John Polkinghorne, *Scientists as Theologians: A Comparison of the Writings of Ian Barbour, Arthur Peacocke, and John Polkinghorne* (London: SPCK, 1996).

For Christians who are interested in the relation between science and Genesis, the most important conversation partners are the kinds of persons mentioned in the preceding paragraphs, not the so-called "new atheists" such as Richard Dawkins, Daniel Dennett, Sam Harris, and Christopher Hitchens.

For most scientists: The Genesis story is at odds with overwhelming empirical evidence and therefore must have some other purpose than a description of how the reality we encounter in the physical world came into existence.

Given that this theology-versus-science controversy pits two disciplines against each other, and that, not surprisingly, each discipline considers its own evidence conclusive and the other evidence illusory, it is understandable that the controversy shows little sign of abating any time soon.

We have, however, adopted neither of these stereotypical positions in this book, nor do we expound an intermediate position such as a "gap theory," a "day-age" approach, or "progressive creation." Instead, we proceed in a relatively unexplored direction that is, in a manner of speaking, at right angles to the range of interpretations outlined above. As a result, the nature of this book and the direction in which it proceeds require some additional explanation, which we provide at the beginning of chapter 1.

Our intention in writing this book is to re-create what the first Hebrew audience heard when Genesis 1 was read or recited to them. We are convinced that what we hear now is profoundly different from what they heard then. We are further convinced that it is well worth the effort to explore some of the reasons why this is the case. This exploration has been initiated in part by some distinctly Adventist advice from nearly 120 years ago:

> There is no excuse for anyone in taking the position that there is no more truth to be revealed, and that all our expositions of Scripture are without an error. The fact that certain doctrines have been held as truth for many years by our people is not a proof that our ideas are infallible. Age will not make error into truth, and truth can afford to be fair. No true doctrine will lose anything by close investigation.[4]

---

4. Ellen G. White, "Christ Our Hope," *Advent Review and Sabbath Herald,*

Not all our readers will agree that the results of our exploration constitute "more truth," but we are convinced that our conclusions deserve to be part of the ongoing conversation about the nature and function of Genesis 1.

Very few books are the product of one or two minds, and certainly this one is not. We are profoundly aware of the contribution of our many conversation partners at Loma Linda and La Sierra universities during the gestation of the ideas contained herein. We are grateful, too, to colleagues here and elsewhere who have critically read various parts or all of the manuscript and made suggestions for its improvement in various ways. We have benefited from the research assistance of librarians at our respective universities. And we will always remember with fondness the hospitality and helpfulness of the staff of Tyndale House, Cambridge, where much of this thinking was initially committed to paper.

Finally, we are indebted to the Adventist Forum for undertaking the publication of this book; to Bonnie Dwyer, executive director of the Forum, for encouragement throughout the process; to Tim Lale for editing assistance that has improved the manuscript in numerous ways; to Heather Langley for creating the cover and interior design as well as the illustrations; and to Ann Parrish for preparing the index.

Brian Bull and Fritz Guy
Loma Linda and Riverside, California

Dec. 20, 1892, 785; repr. *Counsels to Writers and Editors* (Nashville: Southern Publishing Association, 1946), 35.

God said, "Let there be light . . ."
– Gen. 1:3 (OHV)

CHAPTER ONE

TRANSLATING "BACKWARDS"

THE CHALLENGE OF RETRO-TRANSLATION

ALMOST EVERY READER of the Bible would grant that the world in which the first Hebrew audience lived was different from the one we inhabit; after all, did they not live three thousand years ago? This book has been written because the authors are convinced that the differences are even more profound and far-reaching and of a different sort than can be explained simply by the passage of time and by the differences in language and culture.

It is this different world that we explore in this book—the world of Genesis 1. It was a world in which the only known agents responsible for events were God and human beings. Everything that happened was the result of the actions of God or of one or more humans. If the nature of an event excluded an identifiable human cause, then what happened—rain, snow, and babies as well as earthquakes and volcanoes—happened as a direct result of God's actions. Echoes of that world still ring in our ears: not too many years ago, events that insurance companies called "acts of God" were understood to be just that—acts of God.

Those who lived in the world of Genesis 1 attributed to God everything not caused by human beings, but not necessarily in

the sense that we today would call "miracle." They were confident
that God acted *routinely* to ensure that the rain would fall ("until
the day that the LORD sends rain on the earth" [1 Kings 17:14]),[1]
that married women would have babies ("When the LORD saw that
Leah was unloved, he opened her womb" [Gen. 29:31]), and that
snow and frost would fall upon the earth ("To the snow, [God]
says, 'Fall on the earth.' " "By the breath of God ice is given, and
the broad waters are frozen fast" [Job 37:6, 10]).

However, in addition to these ways in which God acted *ordinarily*, God also on occasion acted *exceptionally*. God parted the sea
for the Israelites escaping from Egypt ("At the blast of your nostrils
the waters piled up, the floods stood up in a heap" [Exod. 15:8]),
thundered from a mountain in giving the law ("The appearance of
the glory of the LORD was like a devouring fire on the top of the
mountain" [Exod. 24:17]) and effected the birth of Isaac from a
mother who was well beyond the normal age of childbearing ("I
will give you a son by her" [Gen. 17:16]). What God did routinely we would, today, likely attribute to the laws of nature—the
observed regularities of the natural order—because we now have
such a category; the ancient Hebrews did not. Similarly, if we are
theists, most of what God did exceptionally we would designate as
"miracle." Our distinction between natural and supernatural was
for them simply the distinction between what God did routinely
and what God did exceptionally—but both categories of God's
action were just that—God acting in the ways in which God had
always acted, usually or unusually.

That, however, is not all that needs to be said on the differences between their world and ours. In the world of Genesis 1,

---

1. Unless otherwise noted, throughout this book English quotations
of Gen. 1:1–2:4a, are taken from our own translations, which we have
named the Original Hearers' Version (OHV). Elsewhere, unless otherwise
noted, we have used the New Revised Standard Version (NRSV).

not only were the active agents limited to two—God and human beings—but also, because there were only two kinds of agency in that world (and the ancient Hebrews understood pretty well what human beings could and could not do), "God" was the default explanation whenever "human beings" were reasonably excluded.

This recourse to God as the default explanation of events makes a profound difference between their world and ours. For example, it sometimes made sense for them to deliberately eliminate the possibility of human influence in an event. In so doing they believed that they could access the mind of God; so they "cast lots." They followed a procedure that is unthinkable for us today, employing what we would call a process of chance or randomness in order to exclude human influence—and that, they believed, meant that the event was caused by God. The idea that in casting lots they gained access to the mind of God was accepted as a matter of fact. The Book of Proverbs expresses this understanding explicitly: "The lot is cast into the lap, but the decision is the LORD's alone" (16:33).

Today, in the Western world, we understand earthquakes, tsunamis, and volcances, as well as rain, snow, and babies, as natural happenings. In addition to the personal agency of God and human beings, we conceive of impersonal agency such as that of the natural order when we think we understand the causality involved; when we don't have a clue about the cause of an event, we tend to think of it as the result of "chance." Strictly speaking, chance is not actually a cause; rather it is a category we use when we do not know how to determine a cause to which we can attribute the occurrence of an event.[2]

---

2. Whether or not there are in fact events that actually occur spontaneously—that is, without any cause whatsoever—in the realm of quantum mechanics is a disputed question in theoretical physics and the philosophy of science. The issue is whether the category of chance is epistemological or ontological—that is, a result of the limitation of human knowledge or of the fundamental nature of reality.

When we are faced with some unusual phenomenon, our default explanation is thus to "nature" and then, if necessary, to "chance" or "randomness." Or we may invoke both nature and chance. Thus we employ two additional factors in our understanding of things-that-happen. Whether or not we are believers in God, we now almost never attribute the so-called "acts of God" directly to God; instead we invoke nature and/or chance. Nor can we look on a roll of dice as an indication of God's will; most of us no longer live in a conceptual world where that is possible. That, however, was the world of Genesis 1. If we fail to reckon with that fact and the difference it makes, we will hear the Biblical accounts as very strange indeed.

Is the world of Genesis 1 so far removed from ours that its picture of a Creator God has become null and void, and the remainder of the Bible has become relatively useless? Not at all. The picture of God delineated in Genesis 1, and the actions and motives ascribed to the Creator there, are as true today as they were three thousand years ago. The meaning embodied in the opening words, "In the beginning God . . ." is as profound in the twenty-first century of the present era as it has been for the past three thousand years. Why and how this is the case is the subject of this book, for we believe that in exploring the differences between the world of Genesis 1 and the world of the present lies the possibility of bridging the perceived gulf between Genesis and science.

REENTERING THE WORLD OF GENESIS 1

To really read is to *listen*, to try to hear what the author wants to say. In the case of ancient documents—especially if, like Genesis, they are so familiar to us that we are quite sure we already know what they say—it is extraordinarily difficult to actually listen to the text. Many—maybe most—of us who set out to read Genesis 1 end up doing something very different. We almost inevitably *interrogate* it, in order to extract from the ancient text answers to our current questions, answers with which we have been familiar since childhood. Quite unintentionally, we often act like an attorney interrogating a friendly witness, expecting that the witness will respond with the answers that the attorney wants to introduce as evidence. If we read Genesis in this fashion, however, we have ignored the vast distance that separates the author's awareness, concepts, perspectives, and concerns from our own. Furthermore—and even more objectionably—we will not be listening to the Biblical text to hear what it has to say to us; we will instead be *using* it for our own ends.

This book is an attempt to assist twenty-first-century readers of Genesis 1 to recognize, respect, and finally bridge the cultural and conceptual distance that separates us from the world of Genesis 1. To the extent that we readers truly *listen,* we will experience the distinctiveness (which to many will seem like strangeness) of the text and its message.

However unfamiliar this approach may be, and however challenging to put into practice, it is one that many Bible commentators have long recommended. In regard to the familiar Sermon on the Mount, for example:

> Let us in imagination go back to that scene, and, as we sit with the disciples on the mountainside, enter into the thoughts and feelings that filled their hearts. Understanding what the words of Jesus meant to those who heard them, we may discern in them a new vividness and beauty, and may also gather for ourselves their deeper lessons.[3]

---

3. Ellen G. White, *Thoughts from the Mount of Blessing* (Mountain View, CA: Pacific Press, 1943), 1.

This chapter is a recommendation to follow a similar practice in listening to Genesis 1.

We have at our disposal all of the concepts we need for listening to Genesis 1. The problem is that, by the very fact of living in the modern world, we have too many concepts—more than are necessary, or even helpful. The purpose of this chapter is to introduce and underscore the difficulty of really *listening* to Genesis 1 and hearing it *as it was originally heard.* It is difficult precisely because of our superfluous mental concepts, the implicit understandings with which we think.

Anyone who hears Genesis 1 read or recited will envision the scenes that the words describe—which, of course, was just what the words were intended to accomplish. Unfortunately, whenever we in modern times picture the events of Genesis 1, unless we are extraordinarily intentional about the process, we create mental images quite unlike those that the author of Genesis intended to evoke in the minds of his listeners several thousand years ago. This book is meant to help reduce the probability of that unhelpful outcome.

If a book is going to employ concepts unfamiliar to its readers, it will often begin by listing and explaining the new concepts the readers will encounter. With regard to Genesis 1, however, the process needs to be turned on its head. We are all already equipped with the concepts we need in order to transform the words of Genesis into mental pictures of how everything began. Genesis presents and develops ideas about the origin of every-thing, the Originator of everything, and the place of humanity in the grand scheme of everything. The words in this explanation of beginnings are, in the main, simple and easy to understand. As for the concepts we need to translate these everyday words into mental pictures of God and the results of creation, we most likely acquired them in elementary school.

The formidable challenge that confronts us when we to try to really listen to Genesis 1 is the need to *forget* a number of concepts—to temporarily expunge them from our consciousness, to inactivate them for the duration of the listening process. This is far more difficult than acquiring new concepts. Removing an idea we have employed in our thinking since childhood is close to a "mission impossible." But it is well worth the effort. Without it, Genesis 1, which lies at the heart of our understanding of our place in relation to the rest of the results of Creation, is, although apparently easy to comprehend, almost inevitably misunderstood.

Part of the reason for this misunderstanding is inherent in the process of translating the meaning of the text from Biblical Hebrew into contemporary English. Translators must make a choice of goals for their endeavor—either a translation that is as literal as possible (reproducing the original words, sentence structures, etc., in a different language), or a translation that is as dynamic as possible (conveying the original meaning, feelings, effects, etc.). The numerous English translations of the Bible present a spectrum, with the New American Standard Bible (NASB) toward one end (we will call it the "right" end) and the Contemporary English Version (CEV) at the other (the "left" end). Every version has its values and limitations, and between the ends of the spectrum are many, many translations that are more or less useful in various ways. Off the "left," dynamic end of the spectrum are paraphrases, of which the currently most popular is Eugene Peterson's *The Message*.[4]

In every case, the process of translation (literally, "carrying across") consists of bringing an ancient, foreign text to modern readers. More often than not, this process of "carrying across"

---

4. Eugene Peterson, *The Message: The Bible in Contemporary Language* (Colorado Springs, CO: NavPress, 2002).

is visualized as bringing the Hebrew, Aramaic, and Greek texts forward, increasing their accessibility to the modern reader by updating archaic and now obscure references and concepts in order to make them available to modern sensibilities. We believe, however, that the idea of "carrying across" can just as aptly be applied in the opposite direction and to the reader as well as to the text. So in this chapter our strategy is to advocate a process that we have called retro-translation—carrying modern readers back to an ancient text that is as foreign conceptually as it is linguistically. If this reversed process of "carrying across" successfully transports modern readers *back* to the text, it will help the various other translations succeed in their efforts to carry an ancient text *forward*. Like retrofitting a bridge or a building for seismic purposes, the work of *retro-translation* is intended to complement, not to replace, the work of others.

THE UNIQUENESS OF RETRO-TRANSLATION

Retro-translation is different from the normal process of translation in two significant ways.

In the first place, retro-translation gives overarching importance to the way the Hebrew text actually reads—what it really *said* and initially *meant*. We assume that the author *meant* something in particular by the words he[5] used and the sequence in which he placed them. Of course, the meaning of the words *then* may have been quite different from what we would mean by our own corresponding words *now*. So a retro-translation of Genesis 1 is based on what is sometimes called a "close reading" of the text, taking into account its various peculiarities. For example:

---

5. The Biblical authors were almost certainly male, given the typical gender roles of their times, places, and cultures.

- The text uses a cardinal number ("one") for the first Creation day but uses ordinal numbers ("second," "third," "fourth," "fifth," "sixth," "seventh") for the succeeding days.
- The text is unusually (perhaps tediously) repetitive at several places. "God said, 'Let the land produce vegetation—plants bearing seed and trees with seed-bearing fruit,' and thus it came to be. The land brought forth vegetation—plants bearing seed, and trees with seed-bearing fruit" (1:11, 12).
- The text is typically formulaic, but not always. God is regularly the active agent in the Creation of specific kinds of reality: God "made the vault" (1:7), "made two great lights" (1:15), "brought the great sea monsters into existence, and all kinds of living, moving creatures" (1:21), and "made the different kinds of wild and domestic animals" (1:25). But "the land produced vegetation" (1:12).
- The text suggests that something does not exist until it is mentioned, and that it does exist after it is mentioned. "Water," for instance, existed prior to the Creation process; the text begins with water everywhere as a great abyss (1:2). By contrast, the "greater light" and the "lesser light" did not exist until the fourth day when, according to the text, they were "made" (1:16; not "made visible," as some interpreters have suggested).

In the second place, in determining the intended meaning of the words, the author's own usage as we have it in the text takes priority. Thus in Genesis 1 the word *sky* (*shamayim*) means either the entire visual vault or some portion of it ("God named the vault *sky*"); *land* (*'eretz*) means the dry ground ("God named the dry ground *land*"); *sea* (*yammim*) means the gathered waters, which the author describes as "beneath the sky," distinguishing them from the waters that were kept "above" by the "vault" (*raqia'*). If no definition is provided by the author, the meaning of the word in question is sought first in the remaining introductory section of Genesis (chapters 1–11), then in the Pentateuch and finally in the rest of the Hebrew Bible (the Old Testament).

Carefully observing these principles helps to ensure that nothing in the translation inadvertently conveys to the modern reader a concept that was not present at the time the text was first heard. Indeed, the retro-translation process itself is the embodiment of an attempt to avoid this all-too-frequent anachronism.

This chapter is an invitation to the challenging task of really *listening* to Genesis 1 on its own terms, and thus *hearing* it as nearly as possible in the way the first audiences heard it. Our goal is to "translate" the modern reader of Genesis 1 back to the world of Genesis 1.

THE PROCESS OF RETRO-TRANSLATION

We make four main observations concerning the process of retro-translation:

1. All translation is necessarily imperfect, not only because everything human is imperfect, but also (and more specifically) because no word in one language is perfectly matched by a word in another language.[6] Words acquire and communicate their meanings by virtue of their uses in cultural and linguistic contexts, and these contexts inevitably vary from one culture to another, as well as within a single culture. Furthermore, the uses

---

6. See, for example, Marcia Falk, "Translation as a Journey," in *The Song of Songs: A New Translation and Interpretation* (San Francisco: HarperSanFrancisco, 1990), 91–98.

of words (and therefore the meanings of words) are continually changing. To take an obvious current example: adult Americans remember when the word *gay* referred to a carefree, lighthearted attitude or atmosphere, as in the title of a once widely read book, *Our Hearts Were Young and Gay*.[7] Now, however, gay is used primarily to signify a homosexual orientation, especially of human males.

So the question for those engaged in retro-translation is not "What does this ancient word mean?" but rather the superficially similar but significantly different question, "What *did* this ancient word mean when it was used in this context?" As the saying goes, "Words don't mean what they *say*; they mean what they *mean*." And if we are hearing words from the past, they meant what they meant *then*, not what they mean to us *now*. What the words meant then, like what words mean now, was determined by the community of speaker(s) and hearers.[8] This is, and was, as true for sacred words as for secular words. Even God, in order to communicate successfully, depends on the meanings the hearers understand.

2. Subsequent translations of an important text (like Genesis 1) tend to be remarkably conservative in the sense that they are heavily influenced by previous translations into the same or other languages. Thus modern English translations of the Hebrew Bible (what most Christians know as the Old Testament) are influenced by previous translations into English (going back to John Wycliffe in the fourteenth century), which in turn were influenced by the Latin Vulgate (going back to Jerome in the

---

7. Cornelia Otis Skinner and Emily Kimbrough, *Our Hearts Were Young and Gay* (New York: Dodd, Mead, 1942).

8. Humpty Dumpty's famous assertion, "When I use a word, it means just what I choose it to mean—neither more nor less" (Lewis Carroll, *Through the Looking-Glass, and What Alice Found There* [1871]) expresses a kind of verbal narcissism that is appropriate only if the speaker's intent is catharsis rather than communication.

fourth/fifth centuries), which was influenced by the Greek translations of the Septuagint (going back to the third century BCE).[9]

3. A retro-translation of Genesis 1:1–2:4a attempts to convey to twenty-first-century readers the sense evoked in the minds of those who first listened to this powerful explanation, an explanation that incorporates the qualities of both prose and poetry in a kind of doxology or Creation hymn.[10] Conversely, we have deliberately avoided English words that convey to twenty-first-century readers concepts that were, to the best of our knowledge, not part of the world of Genesis 1 and hence could not have been part of the meaning intended by the author or understood by the audience. Consequently some of the language may seem strange or awkward (or both), and, worst of all, distressingly "un-Biblical," because it is necessary to sacrifice polished English and traditional wording in the interest of retro-translational accuracy. This is, after all, Scripture to which we are listening, and neither familiarity, nostalgia, nor felicity can justify anything less than a sincere effort to really *listen* to it.

4. A retro-translation is not a paraphrase. It is, in fact, the most literal translation of all, in the sense that the Hebrew text has been meticulously reproduced in intelligible English. Where this procedure has, on rare occasions, required an additional

---

9. This influence is evident even in later translations into modern English directly from the best available Hebrew texts. Our example here is the Hebrew word *'eretz*, which, as every first-year Hebrew student knows, means *land*, as in "the land of Egypt" or "the land of Israel" or "the promised land." Occasionally it has a broad meaning, as in the phrase "the whole land." Modern translators of Genesis 1:1, however, persist in rendering *'eretz* as *earth*, which to a modern reader means planet Earth, something it could not have meant to the original hearers of Genesis 1.

10. Other Creation hymns in the Old Testament are Ps. 104 and Prov. 8:22–31. These, as well as the creation narrative in Gen. 2, must be taken into account in the formulation of any fully Biblical doctrine of Creation.

English word to clarify the original meaning, that word is enclosed in square brackets.

THE ORIGINAL HEARERS' VERSION (OHV)

The following translation of Genesis 1:1–2:4a is the result of our best efforts to convey to twenty-first-century readers the "thoughts and feelings that filled [the] hearts" of those who first heard the powerful description of Creation. Because we have attempted to "retro-translate" ourselves and the reader as completely as possible back to the original occasion and milieu of the text, we have not included the usual verse numbers, as they are not part of the original text but a much later addition. The paragraphing is our own addition, reflecting our sense of natural pauses in an oral presentation of this distinctive account of the Creation of the world.

A RETRO-TRANSLATION OF GENESIS 1:1–2:4a

TO BEGIN WITH, God brought into existence the sky and the land. Now [as for] the land, [it] was without form or function, darkness covered the water, and God's Spirit hovered over the surface of the abyss.

God said, "Let there be light"; light came to be, and God saw that the light functioned well. God separated the light from the darkness, and named the light "day" and the darkness "night." There was evening, then dawning—one [Creation] day.

God said, "Let there be a vault within the water, and let it separate the water." God made the vault and separated the water under the vault from the water above the vault, and thus it came to be. God named the vault "sky." There was evening, then dawning—a second [Creation] day.

God said, "Let the water beneath the sky be collected in one place so that dry ground will appear"; and thus it came to be. God named the dry ground "land" and the collected water "sea." God saw that it functioned well.

Then God said, "Let the land produce vegetation—various kinds of plants bearing seed and trees on the land with seed-bearing fruit"; and thus it came to be. The land produced vegetation—various kinds of plants bearing seed and trees with seed-bearing fruit. And God saw that it functioned well. There was evening, then dawning—a third [Creation] day.

God said, "Let there be lights in the vault of the sky to distinguish the day from the night. Let them function as signs—for designated times, for days, and for years. And let them function as lights in the vault of the sky to light up the land." And thus it came to be. God made two great lights—the larger light to dominate the day; the smaller light to dominate the night—as well as the stars. God set them in the vault of the sky to light up the land, and to dominate the day and the night—to separate the light from the darkness. And God saw that it functioned well. There was evening, then dawning—a fourth [Creation] day.

God said, "Let the water produce lots of living creatures, and birds that will fly across the face of the vault of the sky." God brought the great sea monsters into existence, and all kinds of living, moving creatures that the water produces in abundance—and all kinds of birds. God saw that it functioned well. God blessed them: "Be fruitful, multiply, and fill all the seas; and let the birds multiply on the land." There was evening, then dawning—a fifth [Creation] day.

God said, "Let the land produce all kinds of living creatures—domestic animals, crawling things, and wild animals"; and thus it came to be: God made the different kinds of wild and domestic animals and all kinds of crawling things. And God saw that it functioned well.

God said, "Let's make a human being in our image— like us—to be in charge of the fish in the sea, the birds in the air, the wild animals, and the farm animals, as well as all the crawling things." So God brought the human being into existence in his image—in God's own image—male and female. God blessed them and told them, "Be fruitful and multiply, till and tame all the land. Take charge of the fish of the sea, the birds of the air and every living creature that moves on the land."

And God said, "Look, I've given you for food every seed-bearing plant on the face of the land, and every fruit-bearing tree. And I've given the green plants for food to every wild beast, bird, and living, crawling creature." And thus it came to be. God observed everything he had made and saw that indeed it functioned very well. There was evening, then dawning—the sixth [Creation] day.

With that the sky and the land were completed, with all their vast array. God completed his work on the seventh day and on the seventh day he rested. And because he rested on the seventh day from all of his Creation work, God blessed the seventh day and made it sacred.

This is how the sky and the land were brought into existence.

*Then God said, "Let the land
produce vegetation . . ."*

– Gen. 1:11 (OHV)

WHY IT IS WHAT IT IS

SOME EXPLANATIONS AND COMMENTS ABOUT OUR RETRO-TRANSLATION

BEGINNING BELOW, we repeat our Original Hearers' Version of Genesis 1 but with extensive explanatory notes. Readers who are not interested in the details of the translation at this point can pass over this chapter without impairing their understanding of the rest of the book. However, since a particular word or phrase in Genesis 1 is the focus of each of the subsequent chapters, on beginning a new chapter readers may find it helpful to look up that word or phrase here in chapter two.

This time we have included the standard verse numbers in order to facilitate comparison of OHV with other translations. Readers may want to consult various versions, such as the following (listed in chronological order of publication and hereafter identified by initials):

Tyndale's Old Testament (TOT), 1530[1]

---

1. *Tyndale's Old Testament: Being the Pentateuch of 1530, Joshua to 2 Chronicles of 1537, and Jonah,* trans. William Tyndale (New Haven, CT: Yale, 1992).

King James Version (KJV), 1611; standardized text, 1769

Young's Literal Translation (YLT), 1862, 1888, 1897, 2003[2]

American Standard Version (ASV), 1901[3]

Revised Standard Version (RSV), 1952[4]

Jerusalem Bible (JB), 1966[5]

New American Standard Bible (NASB), 1971[6]

Today's English Version (TEV), 1976[7]

New International Version (NIV), 1978[8]

New King James Version (NKJV), 1982[9]

New Jerusalem Bible (NJB), 1985[10]

Tanakh (JPS), 1985[11]

Revised English Bible (REB), 1989[12]

New Revised Standard Version (NRSV), 1989[13]

---

2. Young's Literal Translation (Grand Rapids, MI: Baker, 2003).

3. American Standard Version (Nashville: Thomas Nelson, 1901).

4. Revised Standard Version (New York: National Council of Churches of Christ in the USA, 1952).

5. The Jerusalem Bible (London: Darton, Longman, & Todd, 1966).

6. New American Standard Bible (La Habra, CA: Lockman Foundation, 1960).

7. Good News Bible: Today's English Version (New York: American Bible Society, 1976).

8. The Holy Bible, New International Version (New York: New York Bible Society, 1978).

9. New King James Version (Nashville: Thomas Nelson, 1982).

10. New Jerusalem Bible (New York: Doubleday, 1985).

11. *Tanakh: A New Translation of the Hebrew Scriptures According to the Traditional Hebrew Text* (Philadelphia: Jewish Publication Society, 1985).

12. Revised English Bible with the Apocrypha (New York: Oxford University Press, Cambridge University Press, 1989).

13. New Revised Standard Version (New York: Division of Christian Education of the National Council of Churches of Christ in the United States of America, 1989).

Contemporary English Version (CEV), 1995[14]
Robert Alter, Genesis (RAG), 1996[15]
New Living Translation (NLT), 1999[16]
English Standard Version (ESV), 2001
Today's New International Version (TNIV), 2005[17]
New English Translation (NET), 2005[18]
New English Translation of the Septuagint (NETS), 2007[19]
New International Version (NIV 2011), 2011[20]

A RETRO-TRANSLATION OF GENESIS 1:1–2:4a WITH NOTES

[1]To BEGIN WITH, God *brought into existence* the *sky* and the *land.*

"To begin with"—from the Hebrew word *bereshith,*[21] "in [a] beginning," "beginningly." The Hebrew text does not include a

14. Contemporary English Version (New York: American Bible Society, 1995).
15. Robert Alter, *Genesis: Translation and Commentary* (New York: Norton, 1996).
16. New Living Translation (Carol Stream, IL: Tyndale, 1999).
17. Today's New International Version (Grand Rapids, MI: Zondervan, 2005).
18. http://bible.org/netbible/ (2005).
19. *New English Translation of the Septuagint* (New York: Oxford, 2007).
20. The Holy Bible, New International Version (Colorado Springs, CO: Biblica, 2011).
21. This and subsequent transliterations of Hebrew words follow the academic style of the *SBL Handbook of Style: For Ancient Near Eastern, Biblical, and Early Christian Studies,* ed. Patrick H. Alexander et al. (Peabody, MA: Hendrickson, 1999), 26.

definite article ("the"), nor does the Septuagint, although definite
articles were present in both languages (in contrast to Latin, which
has none). The definite article is added in most English translations, maintaining a tradition going back beyond KJV to TOT, the
first translation of the Pentateuch from Latin into English (1530).

"brought into existence"—from the Hebrew verb *bara'*,
which is usually translated "create[d]." In the Hebrew Bible this
verb's grammatical subject (implied in passive constructions) is
always God. Here in Genesis 1, and often elsewhere, the emphasis
is functional rather than material. Thus the concern is not simply
that something new *exists*, but that new events and processes can
now occur—as the subsequent explanation makes clear.[22]

Here the word *bara'* obviously does not connote *creatio ex
nihilo*, "creation out of nothing." For the Hebrews this concept came
much later, in the intertestamental period. The reality described here
began with water already in existence. The absence of the idea of
creatio ex nihilo from Genesis 1, however, does not imply anything
whatsoever about the theological and philosophical validity and
importance of this idea—only that the questions it raises have to
be decided on other grounds.

"sky"—from the Hebrew noun *shamayim*, usually translated "heaven" or "heavens." This is the dual form of an unused
singular noun, similar to the plural form "mathematics" in English.
Unlike English, however, Hebrew has three noun forms indicating
number: singular (one), dual (two), and plural (three or more).

In our space age, "heavens" inevitably but misleadingly suggests the *universe*, which was entirely unknown to the original
Hebrew listeners. They pictured a vault or dome (see on verse 6
below) that protected the organized Creation from the waters of
chaos (the "abyss"; see on verse 2 below). The sun, moon, and

22. See John H. Walton, *The Lost World of Genesis One: Ancient Cosmology
and the Origins Debate* (Downers Grove, IL: InterVarsity, 2009), 38–46.

stars were set in the "vault."

"land"—from the Hebrew noun *'eretz*, which means "territory," "homeland," as in "the land of Havilah" and "the land of Cush" (Gen. 2:11, 12). "Homeland" is suggested here in an attempt to capture part of the meaning it likely conveyed to its Hebrew hearers—something like that carried by a twentieth-century popular song: "This land is your land; this land is my land. . . . This land was made for you and me."[23] The English translation "earth" goes back beyond KJV to TOT, where Genesis 1:1 reads, "In the beginning God created heaven and earth" (omitting the definite articles that are present in the Hebrew text).

Genesis 1:1 functions as what writing teachers often call a "thesis sentence" for the explanation that follows.

> [2]*Now* the land *was* without form or function; darkness covered the *water;* and God's spirit hovered over the *surface* of the *abyss.*

"Now"—from the Hebrew conjunctive prefix *w*, usually "and," but when connecting clauses, it has a variety of semantic functions, like its English counterpart. It is used, for example, to convey meanings such as these:

- Consequence: "and so" ("I just flew home from London and I am very tired");
- Contrast: "but" ("God is in heaven and we are on earth")
- Chronological sequence: "and then" ("He got up and went to work")
- Introduction: "now" in a nontemporal sense ("And this may seem exaggerated")

---

23. Woody Guthrie, "This Land Is Your Land" (New York: Ludlow Music, 1956).

This versatile word will come up for consideration again in chapters 5, 8, and 10. At this point we note simply that there is no textual or contextual basis for supposing that it introduces a *second* process of creation described in Genesis 1:2–31, separated by an indefinite period of time (as much as 13.7 billion years) from a *first* process of creation mentioned in Genesis 1:1.[24]

"was"—from the Hebrew verb form *yᵉhi*, a past tense of the common, irregular Hebrew verb *hayah,* "to be." In certain contexts this form of the verb can be properly understood to mean "came to be" or "became." This, indeed, is the sense of our OHV translation at the end of this verse, "There was evening, then dawning." Thus this sentence could possibly be translated, "And (then) the land came to be without form or function." This possibility has given rise to the "ruin and restoration" interpretation of Genesis 1, according to which the results of the primordial Creation were destroyed (in whatever way and for whatever reason) and followed by a second Creation, resulting in the world we now inhabit. In chapter 8 we will address this possibility again.

"without form or function"—from the Hebrew adjectival phrase *tohu wabohu* (now often pronounced *tohu vavohu*). REB translates the phrase as "a vast waste"; CEV has "barren, with no form of life." Robert Alter suggests "welter and waste," noting that the phrase "occurs only here and in two later biblical texts that are clearly alluding to this one."[25] OHV's "without form or function" attempts a similar rhythm and assonance and underscores the idea

---

24. This current version of the "gap theory" seems to be motivated by a desire to harmonize Gen. 1 with modern scientific understandings of the size and age of the known universe by interpreting Gen. 1:2–31 as describing only the creation of life on planet Earth. An obvious problem with this proposal is the explicit assertion that on the fourth day God "made [Heb. *'asah,* not "made visible," as sometimes supposed] two great lights . . . as well as the stars" (1:16).
25. RAG, 3.

that God was constituting form out of formlessness and enabling that form to function as God intended. The phrase *tohu wabohu* is the subject of chapter 9.

"water"— from the Hebrew word *mayim*, "water(s)." This is another grammatically dual noun that translates into idiomatic English as singular.

"surface"—from the Hebrew word *panim*, "face." In this context, the word meant "surface." We, with our modern scientific mindset, may wonder how only water and darkness could have a surface, since neither air nor atmosphere yet existed. But the author was not at all concerned with our scientific questions and could hardly be expected to provide answers. Chapter 8 addresses the problems inherent in placing "scientific" demands on Genesis 1.

"abyss"—from the Hebrew word *tehom*, "primeval deep." Modern listeners to the text may picture this as water and darkness "infinite in all directions." For the Hebrews, however, the abstract concept of infinity was still far in the future. For their approximation of infinity they would likely have thought "as countless as the stars of the sky and as measureless as the sand on the seashore" (Jer. 33:22, NIV).

> [3]God said, "Let there be light"; light came to be, [4]and God saw that the light *functioned well*. God separated the light from the darkness, [5]and named the light *"day"* and the darkness "night." There was evening, then dawning—*one [Creation] day*.

"functioned well"—from the Hebrew *tob* (commonly pronounced with a long "o" and a final "v," rhyming with "cove"), an adjective that is usually translated "good." The word *tob*, however, has an extremely wide semantic range, including "pleasant, useful, efficient, beautiful, kind, right, morally good."[26] But

> the most common meaning of *tob* in the OT is utilitarian.
> From the perspective of the suitability of an object or person,
> the focus is on the functional aspect as being in proper order
> or suited for the job. We are thus dealing with 'goodness for
> something,' with a very concrete and tangible meaning in
> the background.
> The approval formula of the Creation Narrative is a
> parade example [German *ein Paradebeispiel*].[27]

The light, like all the other results of Creation activity, functioned as God intended.[28]

However it is translated, the word *tob* does not imply perfection. This common misperception is the result of reading back into the text later Christian theological interpretations.

"**day**"—from the Hebrew noun *yom*. This word has the same

26. Ludwig Koehler and Walter Baumgartner, *Lexicon in Veteris Testamenti Libros* (Grand Rapids, MI: Eerdmans, 1951), 349.

27. I. Höver-Johag, "*tob*," in *Theological Dictionary of the Old Testament*, vol. 5, ed. G. Johannes Botterweck and Helmer Ringgren, trans. David E. Green (Grand Rapids, MI: Eerdmans, 1986), 304. The paragraph continues: "Essential to the interpretation of *tob* is its use with *ra'a*, which means 'see' in the sense of 'regard,' 'examine,' or even 'think proper,' so as to arrive at the conclusion: 'Truly, it is good.' In this way the functionality of the work is emphasized, the fact that the world God has created is 'in good order.' Mesopotamian parallels indicate that the expression 'see that something is good' or 'see how good something is' was used by craftsmen on completion of their work. The utilitarian interpretation is underscored by indicating the functions served by the works of creation. They are good for the purpose for which they were fashioned, without any suggestion of objective evaluation."

28. Compare R. J. Berry, "I Believe in God, Maker of Heaven and Earth," in *Real Scientists, Real Faith*, ed, R. J. Berry (Grand Rapids, MI: Monarch, 2009), 10: "God judged his creation as fit for his purposes."

kind of semantic range as its English counterpart, including such meanings as the period of the sunlight, in contrast to night (as here); a time when significant happenings take place, as in "day of judgment" and "day of the LORD"; and an indefinite period of time (as in Gen. 2:4, 17). "With 2,304 Hebrew occurrences and 16 Aramaic, it is the fifth most frequent noun in the OT" and "is thus by far the most common expression of time."[29] We will discuss this word more extensively in chapter 10.

"one"—from the Hebrew number *'echad.* This is the cardinal number "one" rather than the ordinal number "first," in contrast to the numbering of the next four days ("second," "third," "fourth," "fifth"). Here the author introduces a *Creation* day. It is different from the light-and-warm-hours workday that has just been introduced (see immediately above); this is an evening-dawning (*'ereb-boqer*) day. It is a period of time that begins with *'ereb* and ends with *boqer.* This day proceeds from darkness to brightness, from indistinctness to clarity, from chaos to cosmos, from futility to functionality.

"[Creation] day"—a period of time made significant by the events that transpired during it. As early as the first part of the third century, Origen (185–254 CE) in Alexandria noted the difficulties arising from an attempt to interpret this period as an ordinary twenty-four-hour day: "What man of intelligence, I ask, will consider that the first and second and the third day, in which there are said to be both morning and evening, existed without sun and moon and stars, while the first day was even without a heaven?"[30]

---

29. M. Saebø, "*yom,* II," in *Theological Dictionary of the Old Testament,* vol. 6, ed. G. Johannes Botterweck and Helmer Ringgren, trans. David E. Green (Grand Rapids, MI: Eerdmans, 1990), 13.
30. Origen, *On First Principles* 4.3, 1, trans. G. W. Butterworth (London: SPCK, 1936; New York: Harper and Row, 1966), 288.

A couple of centuries later, Augustine in North Africa regarded the account of a six-day Creation as a temporally expanded narrative for the benefit of unsophisticated readers who could not comprehend the Creation of everything at once. "The days of creation, he suggests, are not periods of time but rather categories in which creatures are arranged by the author for didactic reasons to describe all the works of creation, which in reality were created simultaneously."[31]

The meaning of "[Creation] day" is the subject of chapter 10.

> [6]God said, "Let there be a *vault* within the water, and let it separate the water." [7]God made the vault and separated the water under the vault from the water above the vault, and thus it came to be. [8]God named the vault "sky." There was evening, then dawning—a second [Creation] day.

"vault"—from the Hebrew noun *raqia'*, "dome," "vault." This word comes from the verb *raqa'*, "to beat out," "to stamp." The noun, which occurs nine times in Genesis 1 (verses 6–8, 14, 15, 17, 20) has been translated variously—as "firmament" in TOT and KJV; as "vault" in REB, NJB, TNIV, and NIV 2011; and as "dome" in TEV, NRSV, and CEV. We have used "vault" instead of "dome" because "vault" connotes an interior rather than an exterior perspective, whereas "dome" connotes both; and the original hearers obviously saw the sky only "from the inside."

The translation of *raqia'* as "expanse," going back at least to YLT (1862) and reappearing in NASB, NIV, ESV, and NET, has no linguistic justification, and may be theologically motivated. In Genesis 1 *raqia'* "denotes a stable, solid entity situated above

---

31. John Hammond Taylor, "Introduction," in *St. Augustine: The Literal Meaning of Genesis,* vol. 1, Ancient Christian Writers 41 (Westminster, MD: Newman, 1982), 9.

the earth, which protects the living world from an influx of the waters of chaos. The noun bears the connotation 'compact, firm,' so that translations such as 'expanse' miss the mark."[32] The word also appears in descriptions of Ezekiel's visions (1:22, 23, 25, 26; 10:1), where it describes the foundation of God's throne; in the Psalms (19:1; 150:1); and in the prophecy of Daniel (12:3).

Even if the initial listeners had not heard the noun form *raqia'*, they would have been familiar with the verb form, *raqa'*, "to beat out," as that was the method in common use in local marketplaces where artisans transformed metal ingots into plates and containers. In early Bible times it referred to beating bronze containers into metal plates for an altar covering (Num. 16:38). "Beating out" was also used to transform gold ingots into gold leaf and gold wire or thread (see, for example, Exod. 39:3). We will have more to say about *raqia'* in chapters 3 and 4.

> [9]God said, "Let the water beneath the sky be collected into one place so that *dry ground* will appear"; and thus it came to be. [10]God named the dry ground "land," and the collected water *"sea."* God saw that it functioned well.

"dry ground"—from the Hebrew noun *yabbashah*, often translated "dry land."

"sea"—from the Hebrew plural noun *yamim*, "sea(s)." Like

---

32. M. Görg, *"raqia',"* in *Theological Dictionary of the Old Testament*, vol. 13, ed. G. Johannes Botterweck, Helmer Ringgren, and Heinz-Josef Fabry, trans. David E. Green (Grand Rapids, MI: Eerdmans, 2004), 649.

Compare *Seventh-day Adventist Bible Dictionary*, 350: "Heb. *raqia'*, 'beaten-out (iron) plate,' 'solid vault (of heaven),' 'firmament.' "

See also W. Dennis Tucker, Jr., "Firmament," in *Eerdmans Dictionary of the Bible*: "A thin sheet, similar to a piece of beaten metal, that stretched from horizon to horizon to form the vault of the sky."

the dual nouns *shamayim,* "sky," and *mayim,* "water," this word is non-singular in form but properly translated into English as singular.

> ¹¹Then God said, "Let the land *produce* vegetation— plants bearing seed and trees with seed-bearing fruit"; and thus it came to be. ¹²The land produced vegetation—seed-bearing plants, and trees with seed-bearing fruit. And God saw that it functioned well. ¹³There was evening, then dawning—a third [Creation] day.

"produce"—from the Hebrew verb *sharats,* "swarm forth." The listeners (and presumably also the author) took for granted that life could originate from nonliving matter. So did everyone else for more than two thousand years afterwards. Note that the first listeners did not hear that God "created" vegetation as they did a few sentences later in connection with "the great sea monsters" and "all kinds of birds" (1:21), and for "the different kinds of wild and domestic animals and all kinds of crawling things" (1:25). It seems highly likely, however, that God's creative power was understood (by both the author and the audience) to be involved in the "production" of vegetation and that God approved of what the land "produced."

> ¹⁴God said, "Let there be lights in the vault of the sky to distinguish the day from the night. Let them function as signs—for *designated times,* for days, and for years. ¹⁵And let them function as lights in the vault of the sky to light up the land." And thus it came to be. ¹⁶God made two great lights—the larger light to dominate the day; the smaller light to dominate the night—as well as the stars. ¹⁷God *set* them in the vault of the sky to light up the land, ¹⁸and to dominate the day and the night—to separate the light from the darkness. And God saw that it functioned well.¹⁹There was evening, then dawning—a fourth [Creation] day.

"designated times"—from the Hebrew plural noun *mo'adim*, referring to regular religious festivals; and thence from the verb *ya'ad,* "appoint," "designate." Because the author and the audience calculated time by means of a lunar-solar calendar, they could readily understand the timing of their religious festivals by the phases of the moon and the annual cycles of the sun.

"set"—from the Hebrew verb *nathan,* "give," "place," or "set." Later Hebrews referred to the sun and moon entering through portals in the east and exiting through portals in the west.[33]

> [20]God said, "Let the water produce lots of living creatures, and birds—birds that will fly across the *face* of the vault of the sky." [21]God brought the great *sea monsters* into existence, and all kinds of living, moving creatures that the water produces in abundance—and all kinds of birds. God saw that it functioned well. [22]God blessed them: "Be fruitful, multiply, and fill all the seas; and let the birds multiply on the land." [23]There was evening, then dawning—a fifth [Creation] day.

"face"—from the plural noun *panim,* as in verse 2. KJV translated this as "open firmament," and some later translations have followed suit.

"sea monsters"—a kind of reality also mentioned in Job 26:12; Psalm 74:12–14; 89:8–10; and Isa. 51:9, 10, where they are designated collectively as "Rahab," "Leviathan," or "dragons." The point here is that these creatures were not preexisting opponents of God (as in contemporary pagan mythology) but were themselves products of God's creativity.

---

33. See *The Book of Enoch the Prophet,* trans. R. H. Charles (Boston: Weiser, 2003), 72–76.

²⁴God said, "Let the land produce every kind of *living creature*—domestic animals, crawling things, and wild animals"; and thus it came to be: ²⁵God made the different kinds of wild and domestic animals and all kinds of crawling things. And God saw that it functioned well.

"living creatures"—from the Hebrew *nephesh chayyah*, "living soul," as in Genesis 2:7.

²⁶God said, "Let's make a human being in our image—like us—to be in charge of the fish in the sea, the birds in the air, the wild animals, and the farm animals, as well as all the crawling things." ²⁷So God brought the human being into existence in his image—in God's own image—male and female. ²⁸God blessed them and told them, "Be fruitful and multiply, till and tame all the land. Take charge of the fish of the sea, the birds of the air and every living creature that moves on the land."
  ²⁹And God said, "Look, I've given you for food every seed-bearing plant on the face of the land, and every fruit-bearing tree. ³⁰And I've given the green plants for food to every wild beast, bird, and living, crawling creature." And thus it came to be. ³¹God observed everything *he* had made, and saw that indeed it functioned very well. There was evening, then dawning—*the sixth [Creation] day*.

"he"—Without implying that God is, in fact, male, we have followed the Hebrew text where it refers to God with masculine pronouns.

"the sixth [Creation] day"—This is the first time this Creation account specifies a day by the use of the definite article *ha*, "the." This usage suggests that the author was bringing to completion his account of the six Creation days. The account began with the definition of "*one* day"; progressed through "*a* second," "*a* third," "*a* fourth," and "*a* fifth day"; and then ended at the close of "*the* sixth [Creation] day."

> ²:¹With that the sky and the land were completed, with all their *vast array*. ²And on the seventh day God *completed* the work he did, and on the seventh day he rested. ³And because he rested on the seventh day from all of his Creation work, God blessed the seventh day and made it sacred.

"vast array"—from the Hebrew plural noun *tsabaoth*, "retinues," "multitudes." Here "all their vast array" (as in NIV and TNIV) means everything that the world of the first listeners contained.

"completed"—from the Hebrew irregular verb *yakal*, "complete," "finish." The discrepancy between the implication in 2:1 that Creation was completed with the *sixth* day, and the explicit assertion in 2:2 that Creation was completed on the *seventh* day has understandably troubled many readers. The Hebrew verbs in the two sentences are in fact identical. Some translators have interpreted the text to read "By the seventh day God had finished the work he had been doing" (NIV, TNIV); but the Hebrew text clearly reads, "On the seventh day God completed the work he did." Jewish tradition has long recognized this issue and suggested that on the seventh day God created rest, *menuha*.[34]

> ⁴These are the *origins* of *the sky and the land* when they were brought into existence.

---

34. See Abraham Joshua Heschel, *The Sabbath: Its Meaning for Modern Man* (New York: Farrar, Straus, 1951), 22, 23.

"origins"—from the Hebrew plural noun *toledoth,* "genera-tions." This word appears ten more times in Genesis,[35] and in every instance introduces a list of descendents. This is obviously not its function here, even if it is regarded as an introduction to what follows in chapters 2 and 3 (which in our judgment it is not) rather than a conclusion to what has preceded it (which we believe to be the case).[36] This is one reason for including this sentence with Genesis 1 rather than with what follows in Genesis 2–3, in spite of the obvious introductory function of the word *toledoth* elsewhere in Genesis.

"the sky and the land"—echoes Genesis 1:1, "To begin with, God brought into existence the sky and the land." Sharing the actual language—"sky" (*shamayim*), "land" (*'eretz*), and "brought into existence" (*bara'*)—the two sentences functioned as verbal "bookends" for those who heard this account of Creation. This is a second reason for associating this sentence with what precedes rather than what follows.

A third reason, decisive in itself although overlooked surpris-ingly often,[37] is that Genesis 2–3 does not in fact describe the

---

35. Gen. 5:1; 6:9; 10:1; 11:10, 27; 25:12, 19; 36:1, 9; 37:2. See also Num. 3:1; Ruth 4:18; 1 Chron. 1:29.

36. See, for example, Walter Brueggemann, *Genesis,* Interpretation: A Bible Commentary for Teaching and Preaching (Atlanta: John Knox, 1982), 22, 24, 29, 35, 38, 40, where Gen. 2:4a is affirmed as the conclusion of the first Creation account but not argued; and Laurence A. Turner, *Genesis,* Readings: A New Biblical Commentary (Sheffield, U.K.: Sheffield Academic, 2000), 25, 26, where this view is briefly explained.

37. This consideration is typically ignored by those who regard Gen. 2:4a as the beginning of the narrative that follows. See, for example, the otherwise careful discussions by Umberto Cassuto, *A Commentary on the Book of Genesis, Part I: From Adam to Noah* (Jerusalem: Magnes Press/Hebrew University, 1961, 1978); C. John Collins, *Genesis 1-4: A Linguistic, Literary, and Theological Commentary* (Phillipsburg, NJ: P & R, 2006), 40–42. On the basis of the presence of the *toledoth* formula,

creation of "the sky and the land," but rather (a) the creation of the human male and female, and (b) their disobedience and its consequences.

A fourth reason is that Genesis 2:4b actually introduces another Creation account: "In the day YAHWEH God made land and sky, no shrub was yet in the land. . . ." Note (1) the name YAHWEH,[38] which does not appear in Genesis 1; (2) the reversed order of "land" and "sky"; and (3) the lack of a definite article, "the," with either "land" or "sky." These verbal variations, minor in themselves, cumulatively confirm the inclusion of Genesis 2:4a as the ending of the Creation account of Genesis 1 rather than the beginning of the Creation account of Genesis 2.

Bruce K. Waltke, with Cathi J. Fredricks, *Genesis: A Commentary* (Grand Rapids, MI: Zondervan, 2001), 79, labels Gen. 2:4–4:26 "The Account of the Heavens and the Earth," in spite of the fact that its contents are immediately described as "Humanity on probation," "The Fall and its consequences," and "The escalation of sin in the line of Cain" (79, 80).
38. Throughout this book we put the name YAHWEH in small capital letters to reflect the ancient Hebrew reverence for the personal divine name.

God named the dry ground "land"
and the collected water "sea."

– Gen. 1:10 (OHV)

CHAPTER THREE

"SKY," "LAND," AND "VAULT"

MENTAL PICTURES THEN VERSUS NOW

THE TRADITIONAL WORDS with which the majestic narrative of Genesis 1 unfolds evoke in our minds different pictures from those evoked in the minds of the first audience three millennia (or longer) ago. We are not going to engage the scholarly discussion of the authorship of Genesis 1, because that issue is not relevant to the purposes of this book. Genesis has been traditionally but not Scripturally attributed to Moses (as reflected in the titles of the "Books of Moses" in KJV), who lived well over a millennium before the birth of Christ; but the text as it has come to us seems clearly to reflect the involvement of later authors or editors.[1]

The pictures in our minds are different from those of the first listeners because we do not understand the created reality we have encountered in the same way the first listeners understood the reality they had encountered. This difference in

---

1. The author is now often identified by scholars as Priestly (or simply P), one of four sources of the Pentateuch according to the "documentary hypothesis": J (for Jahvist or Yahwist), E (for Elohist), D (for Deuteronomist), and P (for Priestly).

understanding comes from the fact that we have an accumulation of information they did not have and could not have had. As a result of this additional information, we employ concepts that are different from theirs.

So, even though we have words that correspond (more or less roughly) to theirs—our *sky* corresponds to their *shamayim* and our *land* to their *'eretz*—we hear the narrative of Creation in Genesis 1 very differently from the way they heard it. The difference between the way they thought about it and the way we think about it is so great that they and we can seem to be living in significantly different intellectual universes.

This divide in concepts and understanding is actually a yawning chasm, and we will spend most of this book exploring its extent and implications. Our exploration can begin at no better place than with the opening line of Genesis 1, familiar from KJV and many modern translations (NASB, NIV, NLT, etc.): "In the beginning God created the heavens and the earth." Recognizing that they thought of "heavens" and "earth"—and, while we are at it, "firmament"—more as "sky," "land," and "vault," respectively, will take us a long way forward on our journey.

The task we have undertaken—to really *listen* to Genesis— is deceptively difficult, because we have to do more than simply acknowledge the obvious—that their "sky and land" was very different from our "universe," even though by these different terms both they and we are referring to all known created reality—that is, all known reality other than God. If we are to really *hear* Genesis 1, it will be necessary for us to experience their "world" as much as we can, trying to actually live in it for at least the time it takes to read carefully the first Genesis narrative of Creation.

TWO ACCOUNTS

To begin the task of carefully reading (and listening to) Genesis 1:1–2:4a, it is important to recognize that, along with the other Creation passages in the Old Testament, there is a second Genesis account of Creation; and that the two accounts, while theologically complementary, are significantly different.

For one thing, the literary form is different. Genesis 1 sounds like a carefully structured hymn of six stanzas, followed by a concluding final stanza. The six stanzas are characterized by recurring language:

- "God said, 'Let [something happen]' " (1:3a, 6a, 9a, 11a, 14, 15a, 20, 24a, 26)
- "[Something] came to be" (1:3b, 7b, 9b, 11b, 15b, 24b, 30b)
- "God made" or "brought into existence" (1:7a, 16, 21a, 25a, 27)
- "God saw that [something] functioned well" (1:4, 10b, 18b, 21b, 25b, 31a)
- "God named" (1:5a, 8a, 10a)
- "There was evening, then dawning . . . day" (1:5b, 8b, 13, 19, 23, 31b).

Genesis 2, by contrast, is a straightforward narrative, without the structured repetition.

For another thing, the order of Creation events is different. In Genesis 1 God creates vegetation, then birds and fish, then animals, and finally male and female humanity. But in Genesis 2:4b–25, which is the first part of a two-chapter narrative of the Creation of humanity and the disastrous results of human sin, God forms a human male before there is vegetation; he then forms animals and birds, and finally a human female. The divergent sequences are typically harmonized (often unconsciously) by revising the order of events in Genesis 2 to fit the order of Genesis 1.[2]

For a third thing, God is very differently involved in the process of Creation. In Genesis 1, God is pictured as totally transcendent, speaking a creative word, "Let there be [some particular reality]. . . ," as a result of which the designated reality comes into existence. This is sometimes called "fiat Creation," from the Latin *fiat,* "let there be." In the narrative of Genesis 2, by contrast, God actually *forms* the human male from soil and later takes one of the male's ribs as material from which to construct his female counterpart.

For a fourth thing, the Creator is differently identified. In Genesis 1, God is simply *'elohim,* "God." In Genesis 2, God is YAHWEH *'elohim,* usually translated "LORD God," using the sacred personal Hebrew name of God, which was probably derived from the Hebrew equivalent of the verb *to be* and may have implied ultimate reality. This name of God was regarded as so holy that pious Jews from the intertestamental period onward never pronounced it aloud but substituted the word *'adonai,* "Lord."[3]

---

2. An apparently deliberate attempt at harmonization is the translation of Gen. 2:8a as "Now the LORD God had planted a garden in the east, in Eden" and 2:19a as "Now the LORD God had formed out of the ground all the beasts of the field and all the birds of the air" (NIV; similarly TNIV and NIV 2011). While the use of the pluperfect tense instead of the simple past tense (NRSV, etc.) is theoretically permissible because Biblical Hebrew lacks an explicit pluperfect, it is justified in these instances only on the prior theological assumption that the two narratives *must* exhibit the same sequence.

3. The consonants of the divine name YAHWEH (*YHWH,* known as the Tetragrammaton), when combined with the vowels of the word *'adonai* in medieval Hebrew manuscripts of the Bible, produce the hybrid English

For a fifth thing, the initial, pre-Creation conditions are very different. In Genesis 1 there is watery chaos accompanied by wind (1:2); but in Genesis 2 water is scarce, with desertlike conditions (2:5). Furthermore, in Genesis 1 water is a threat against which the heavenly vault is protection (1:6, 7); but in Genesis 2 water is a source of life by means of a river that flows out of Eden and divides into four branches (2:10–14).[4]

Careful attention to the actual Biblical text thus makes it impossible to sustain the popular assumption that Genesis 2:4b–25 is simply a continuation of Genesis 1:1–2:4a. Both narratives are explanations of Creation, and both emphasize the uniqueness of humanity within the whole created reality; but they are clearly different narratives.

IDENTIFYING AND "ELIMINATING" CONCEPTS

Really *listening* to Genesis 1 necessarily involves a procedure to which our minds are quite unaccustomed: the identification and suspension of some of the concepts with which we think. We are familiar enough with the sensation of *aha!* at the moment when we suddenly grasp a new idea, a new concept, a new way of seeing the world. But for the task of really *listening to* and *hearing* Genesis, we need to undertake the quite strange and uncongenial task of temporarily suspending some of our intuitive concepts, "forgetting" a number of our taken-for-granted understandings of reality. We need to leave our own mental world and, for a time, inhabit the "lost world" of Genesis 1.[5] This is obviously a major

---

term *Jehovah.*
4. See Terence E. Fretheim, *Creation, Fall, and Flood: Studies in Genesis 1-11* (Minneapolis: Augsburg, 1969), 45–47.
5. John H. Walton, *The Lost World of Genesis One.*

challenge, for in hearing Genesis 1 we need to avoid the ever-present hazard of imposing *our* picture of the world on the Genesis text and thus ensuring that we will "find" in Genesis what we know must be there. This is an equal-opportunity hazard, beset-ting many devout scholars as well as most casual readers.

In listening to Genesis 1, the danger is especially great at the beginning. By the end of the first ten verses, the listener, ancient or modern, has formed one of two kinds of mental pictures of what the author is describing. On the one hand, we can be firmly ensconced in the world of the author, viewing reality through his eyes and seeing what he[6] saw in the creative works of God.

> [1]To BEGIN WITH, God brought the sky and the land into existence. [2]Now [as for] the land [, it] was without form or function, darkness covered the water, and God's Spirit hovered over the surface of the abyss.
>
> [3]God said, "Let there be light"; light came to be. . . . [4]God separated the light from the darkness, [5]and named the light "day" and the darkness "night". [6]God said, "Let there be a vault within the water, and let it separate the water."
>
> [7]God made the vault and separated the water under the vault from the water above the vault, and thus it came to be. [8]God named the vault "sky."
>
> [9]God said, "Let the water beneath the sky be collected in one place so that dry ground will appear"; and thus it came to be. [10]God named the dry ground "land" and the collected water "sea."

---

6. Since it is more than likely that all, or at least most, of the contributors to the text of Genesis 1 were male, we will continue to use masculine pronouns to refer to the author(s) and/or editor(s).

Or, on the other hand, we can remain in our twenty-first-century mindset, picturing the creative works of God through the lens of the Hubble Space Telescope.[7] Unfortunately, it is the latter situation that almost always overtakes us when we listen to Genesis 1. This is the inevitable outcome unless we work very hard to move from an *intellectual recognition* of the ancient world to an *experiential understanding* of it.

Really *listening* to Genesis is indeed difficult, but it is not impossible. So we will do our best.

"SKY"

What mental picture was evoked by the word *shamayim* ("sky") in the minds of those who first listened to the Creation account in Genesis 1? This word is almost always translated "heavens" or "heaven." As we mentioned in chapter 2, this word is dual in form but has a singular, collective meaning. Dual or plural nouns as collectives occur commonly in Hebrew. In Genesis 1 the words *mayim* ("water") and *yammim* ("sea") are examples of this use. The sense is that of an extensive, even immense, reality. On occasion we achieve the same end in modern English by using the plural form when we are talking astronomically ("the starry heavens"). Typically, however, we use the singular form when we are talking theologically ("God is in heaven").

The Jewish scholars who produced the Septuagint, a collection of Greek translations of the Hebrew Bible from the third to the first centuries before the common era, heard the author

---

7. Named in honor of the American astronomer Edwin Hubble (1889–1953), who confirmed the existence of other galaxies besides the Milky Way as well as the expansion of the universe, the Hubble Space Telescope was carried into orbit by a space shuttle in 1990.

of Genesis 1 speaking of *ouranos*, the space far above the earth—the sky or heaven. Jerome (ca. 347–420 CE), translating the Hebrew Bible into Latin, similarly heard *caelum*, the sky or heaven. But the translators of early English Bibles, beginning with William Tyndale (1530) and including the historically influential KJV (1611), evidently heard only "heaven" or "heavens." Because these early and influential English translators did not hear "sky," virtually all subsequent translators haven't heard "sky" either.

To assist us in really *listening* to the text, and understanding what the first hearers of Genesis 1 heard in the word *shamayim*, we will need to construct a miniature world-of-the-ancient-Middle-East. We will benefit substantially from this exercise because we no longer live in that world. When the ancient Hebrews looked at the sky they saw something that we no longer see—a firmament, a heavenly vault, something solid and protective over their heads. To help us to recapture their experience, a "visual aid" is in order! This device will aid us immeasurably in understanding what it was like to live in that world. When the ancient Hebrews looked at the sky, they saw overhead something like an enormous inverted bowl. A hemispherical copper bowl will get us nicely started, and fortunately, suitably shaped containers are readily available from cookware and kitchen suppliers because copper bowls are ideal for whipping egg whites into maximum frothiness. (They work so well because of the stabilizing effect of copper ions on the air trapped in the beaten egg whites.) The copper hemisphere should now be lined with heavy, dark-blue fabric. If we are really "into" the project at this juncture, we can stick a star or two and maybe a crescent moon to the inner aspect of the bowl lining.

To complement the "sky" and complete our world-of-the-ancient-Hebrews in miniature, we need some "land." We will return to its construction and the reasons why the "land" should fit snugly into the circumference of the "sky" in the next section of this chapter. Now, however, we should picture ourselves as miniature observers looking up at the inside of an immense bowl with the sun, moon, and stars set into it as it turns majestically overhead.

Unfortunately, in today's world this experience of standing under the night sky and seeing it as a vast heavenly bowl is very difficult to re-create for two reasons. One problem is light pollution: ever since the invention of the electric light, the night sky almost everywhere is polluted by stray illumination from streetlights in towns and cities. The other problem comes from the fact that we live in a post-Hubble universe: when we look out at the night sky and see shimmering points of light, in our mind's eye we picture them as suns much like our own (except that many of them are much bigger), and we may even picture them as galaxies. If we remember some astronomy, we know that we are seeing just a small sampling of a hundred billion galaxies, each containing something like a hundred billion stars, and probably as many planets more or less like those in our solar system.

The point is that we do not—and cannot—see simple points of light in a vast heavenly bowl rotating above our heads. Despite what our eyes are telling us, we cannot do this because we know that we are the ones who are moving (along with the other planets going around our sun) against a background of "fixed stars." Perhaps we can achieve some small sense of the ancient Hebrews' nightly experience by the simple expedient of taking a camera to a place where light pollution is minimal, aiming it at a portion of the sky that includes the North Star, and leaving the lens open for several hours. If we do this with appropriate attention to f-stops and the like, the stars will leave "star trails," segments of the circular path that each star follows on its apparent journey through the heavens. For those stars near to the North Star, these "star trails" describe a segment of a tight circle whose radius is the distance between that star and the North Star. For the stars farther away, the "star trail" also describes the segment of a larger circle, but one that, if it is continued all the way around, will at some point be interrupted by the horizon.

We can imagine looking up at this grand spectacle of stars pursuing their course through the sky, all the while apparently guided by a North Star night after night. That was the *shamayim* when Genesis 1 was first spoken. And, if the dates given to the megalithic structures in England and Ireland are at all accurate, even as Genesis was being composed, that view had already been the "sky" of ancient humanity for a couple of thousand years.

"LAND"

Beginning with the earliest English translations of the Bible, the word *'eretz* has been translated as "earth." But whenever the word *earth* is used in a modern astronomical or cosmological context, we hear it as "planet Earth." Since the moon landings in the 1960s and 70s, it is a rare person who does not, on hearing "earth," imagine a blue sphere outlined against the blackness of space, swathed in clouds and rising over the barren wasteland of the moon's surface. But picturing planet Earth as seen from space has only been possible for a few decades. It is true that Galileo's observations through his telescope in the early 1600s, plus his defense of his view of the universe,[8] gave his contemporaries access to the notion of Earth as a planetary body that circled a stationary sun; but that was only a few hundred years ago.

The people of Bible times, if we are to judge by the Biblical

---

8. Galileo Galilei (1564–1642), *Dialogue Concerning the Two Chief World Systems* (1632).

references to *'eretz*, by which they meant first of all the land where they lived (recall chapter 2), pictured it as a relatively flat surface, the center of the created reality. Here is "the earth" as reconstructed in a comparatively recent Bible dictionary:

> The ancient Hebrews imagined the world as flat and round, covered by the great solid dome that was held up by mountain pillars (Job 26:11; 37:18). Above the dome and under the earth was water, divided by God at creation (Gen. 1:6, 7; compare Ps. 24:2; 148:4). The upper waters were joined with the waters of the primordial deep during the Flood; the rains were believed to fall through windows in the firmament (Gen. 7:11; 8:2). The sun, moon, and stars moved across or were fixed in the firmament (Gen 1:14-19; Ps. 19:4, 5). Within the earth lay Sheol, the realm of the dead (Num. 16:30-33; Is. 14:9, 15).[9]

The "earth" was immovable. Indeed, immobility, fixedness, was its preeminent characteristic. That the "earth" was fixed and would never—*could* never—be moved was evidence of God's sovereignty and trustworthiness (Ps. 104:5).

Furthering our attempt to experience the world of the ancient Hebrews, we need to complement our bowl-shaped sky with corresponding land. A disk of wood, covered with cork and painted green, makes a promising start. For proper effect the disk should fit snugly inside the hemispherical bowl, with a diameter only slightly smaller than the rim of the bowl. This is to enable the sky and the land to meet at the perimeter, the horizon. For those who first listened to Genesis 1, it was in this way that the waters of chaos above were held away from the

---

9. Quoted from the explanation of the drawing under "firmament" in *Harper's Dictionary of the Bible*, ed. Paul J. Achtemeier (San Francisco: Harper and Row, 1985), 309.

land, which was thus sheltered and protected within our inverted bowl.

With the addition of a range of mountains along one edge,
some animals and a few trees, and perhaps a lake or the edge of a
sea, our model of the ancient Hebrew world-as-they-experienced-
it is complete.

"VAULT"

Inextricably tied up with the "sky" and the "land" was the
"vault" or "firmament." The word *firmament* is familiar to most
adult Christians from the traditional KJV language of Genesis 1
(although it does not appear in any recent English translation;
see again chapter 2). It is also familiar to many from the parallelism that begins Psalm 19 (KJV): "The heavens declare the
glory of God; and the firmament sheweth his handywork."

"Firmament" is the English form of the Latin *firmamentum*,
meaning literally a strengthening support or prop. This word
from classical Latin was used in the Old Latin translations (early
third century) of Genesis from the Greek text of the Septuagint
rather than directly from the Hebrew Bible. The Greek word
was *stereoma*, referring to something solid. When, in the late
fourth century of the Christian era, Jerome went back to the
Hebrew text and translated it directly into Latin in what later
became part of the standard version known as the Vulgate, he
retained *firmamentum* to catch the meaning of the Hebrew *raqia'*.

The noun *raqia'* comes from the verb *raqa'*, which occurs
in several places in the Hebrew Bible.[10] Whenever it occurs, its
meaning is clear: to pound some material, often metal, into thin
sheets (or even thread) or to take an ingot of metal (such as

---

10. See, for example, Exod. 39:3; 2 Sam. 22:43; Jer. 10:9.

bronze) and pound it into a container by shaping the metal as the pounding produces a sheet. Gold is the most malleable of metals; it responds to pounding more readily even than bronze and can be transformed into very thin sheets indeed. These sheets are so tenuous that they are often described as "gold leaf." Thus, *raqa'* occurs in connection with the production of gold leaf used to cover portions of the tabernacle: "Gold leaf was hammered out and cut into threads" (Exod. 39:3).

To an early Hebrew listener who was familiar with the sight of artisans hammering out bronze bowls or making gold jewelry in the local bazaar, the meaning of *raqia'* was immediately evident. That, however, is not the case for us. To our ears, *firmament* is almost meaningless. Jerome did manage to catch the idea of "firm," the idea that this object, whatever it was, had heft and substance like a metal dome, but that is about all. In English as opposed to Hebrew, the word fails to denote anything in particular. But to those who first heard Genesis 1, *raqia'* immediately brought to mind the verb *raqa'*, with which they were familiar. The word *raqa'* would, in turn, bring to mind the stories they had heard from childhood of the gold and precious stones brought out of Egypt during the Exodus and how that precious metal was used during the construction of the tabernacle in the wilderness.

For the modern English hearer of the text of Genesis, the word *vault* comes closest to matching the mental picture of the ancient Hebrew listeners. Those of us who are not professional astronomers or space scientists, and whose knowledge of cosmology is limited to an occasional planetarium visit, still think in terms of a sky *dome* or *vault*. Indeed, even today, astronomers locate stars by placing them on the inside surface of an imaginary sphere surrounding the earth; the declination of a star is its latitude on that imaginary sphere. Professional astronomers sometimes use other obscure terms like "right ascension" when talking with the rest of us, but many of the terms they use even when talking among themselves refer metaphorically to an imaginary sphere surrounding the earth.

What mischief did Galileo wreak when he dislodged the earth from the center of everything! He left us as lonely wanderers in a universe from which the enchantment had fled, a universe with no place for a "firmament," much less a "vault." Where that "vault" was to be found and why it was important, we will consider next.

*God said, "Let there be a vault . . .
and let it separate the water."*
– Gen. 1:7 (OHV)

CHAPTER FOUR

"THE VAULT OF THE SKY"

CRITICAL FOR CREATION

IN LISTENING to Genesis 1, the challenge is especially great at the beginning. By the end of the first ten verses, the listener, ancient or modern, has formed one of two kinds of mental picture (sometimes very detailed) of what the author is describing.

Ideally, we, modern readers though we are, will be firmly ensconced in the world of the author, viewing it through his eyes and seeing what he saw in the creative works of God. So what did those first hearers picture—how does the "vault" relate to the "sky," the "land," and the other major elements in the opening verses of the Bible? Why, for instance, is "sky" joined at the hip with "vault" four times in the phrase, "vault of the sky" (verses 14, 15, 17, 20)? Why was the concept of an encircling vault so important to the author and his listeners? Even more surprising, how could a vault-that-overarches be critical for creation?

Genesis 1 is a carefully structured composition. Its artistry was recognized by medieval Christians, who "distinguished the work of separation (days 1-3) from the work of adornment (days

4-6)."[1] These two phases of creative activity may be better characterized as "giving form" and "assigning function," since they remedy, respectively, the pre-Creation conditions of "without form [Heb. *tohu*] or function [*bohu*]." The symmetry of the three pairs of days has been noted since the late eighteenth century: corresponding to light (day 1) are the lights (day 4); corresponding to the sky and the waters under the sky (day 2) are birds and fish (day 5); and corresponding to land and vegetation (day 3) are land animals, including human beings, and the gift of food (day 6).[2]

In Genesis 1, "vault" (*raqiaʿ*) occurs only in the first part of the Creation narrative, the phase during which God "gave form" (days 1–3). During the second phase, when God "assigned function" (days 4–6), the place of "vault" was taken by "sky" (*shamayim*). The combined designation "vault of the sky" occurs during the transition between the two phases.

Those of us who inhabit university environments naturally think of academic analogies. In this case, we suggest that the expression "the vault of the sky" is much like "the ceremony of graduation." In each case the prepositional phrase modifies the preceding noun: "of the sky" and "of graduation" explain, respectively, what kind of vault and what kind of ceremony is meant. Just as we commonly say "graduation ceremony," we can say "sky vault" (or "sky-vault"). But we can also understand the prepositional phrases as appositives or synonyms of the nouns: just as we can logically think of "the ceremony of graduation" as "the ceremony that is graduation," so we can logically think of "the vault of the sky" as "the vault that is the sky."

---

1. Henri Blocher, *In the Beginning: The Opening Chapters of Genesis* (Downers Grove, IL: InterVarsity, 1984), 51.
2. Blocher credits this observation to the German philosopher Johann Gottfried von Herder (1744–1803).

A way of emphasizing the importance of a concept to a speaker, an importance the speaker hopes will be recognized by the audience, is repetition—a way that is still rhetorically effective. For this reason it is worthwhile to consider the number of times various words are used in Genesis 1:

- God (*'elohim*)   32 times
- land (*'eretz*)   20 times
- sky (*shamayim*)   12 times
- vault (*raqia'*)   8 times

From this table it seems reasonable to conclude that Genesis 1 is first and foremost about God the Creator; secondly it is about God's creation of the sky and the land (and their contents); and thirdly it is about the vault—the *raqia'*.

But there is more to be said about this. Although "vault" by itself runs a poor fourth in the number of times it was heard by the first listeners, that is because in the second part of the narrative its place is taken by "sky." If the instances of "vault," "vault of the sky," and "sky" are totaled, then the vault of the sky is important indeed. In the part of Genesis 1 that describes God giving form to Creation, "vault" is second in importance only to the Creator. Through the first three creation days (Gen. 1:1–13) the vocabulary statistics are as follows:

- God (*'elohim*)   13 times
- vault (*raqia'*)   5 times
- light (*'or*)   4 times
- seas (*mayim*)   3 times
- abyss, waters of chaos (*tehom*)   3 times

After verse 13, "vault" occurs four more times but always in the combined form, "vault of the sky":

- "God said, 'Let there be lights in the vault of the sky' " (1:14)
- " 'Let them function as lights in the vault of the sky' " (1:15)
- "God set them in the vault of the sky" (1:17)
- " 'birds that will fly across the face of the vault of the sky' " (1:20).

Clearly the "sky," "land," and "vault" were intended to be of great importance to those who first heard Genesis 1; and it follows that they should be important to us if we are going to really *hear* Genesis.

That the "vault" was not just a visual sensation but something a great deal more significant and substantial was surely clear to those who first heard Genesis 1. But what they pictured is so foreign to our understanding that we can read Genesis indefinitely and never once tumble to what the author was conveying with the assertion that "the vault . . . separated the water under the vault from the water above the vault, and thus it came to be. God named the vault 'sky' " (1:7, 8a). What was described here was something that could protect the created reality from the water(s) of chaos above.[3]

The narrative is clear: God created something that "separated the waters under the vault from the waters above the vault," and the rest of Creation took place within the protected confines of that vault.

---

3. The "water(s) under the vault" presumably included both the "sea" and the "water under the land [*'eretz*]"—the latter appearing again in the Hebrew Bible most famously in the second of the Ten Commandments, where it was considered to be the home of creatures that might entice the Israelites into idolatry (Exod. 20:4).

DISAPPEARANCE OF THE VAULT

A simple experiment will confirm that the vault, which was an essential element to those who first heard Genesis 1, has become practically invisible, especially to those who have grown up with the "firmament" of KJV. The next time you are in a group familiar with the Bible—people who, with only an occasional assist, could repeat the first twenty or so verses of Genesis from memory—ask them what topic (other than God) was most essential to the telling of what happened during the first three days of Creation. Then propose a simple ground rule for analyzing the text—that the topic of greatest importance is the one mentioned most often.

How many Biblically literate respondents will get the answer right? Usually none! Even though they may be able to repeat much of Genesis from memory, it is a very unusual person who thinks of "vault" (or "firmament") when questioned in this way. The reason is at the heart of the difficulty we all have in really *hearing* Genesis: we hear only what we can categorize and place in context. We can only think about entities that fit into our explanatory concepts.

Neither a substantial "vault" nor a "firmament" finds any place in the modern mind; particularly not a "vault" that protects the rest of created reality from the waters of chaos above. If we imagine ourselves as space travelers on board the first flight of a rocket ship catering to space tourists, we picture leaving the earth's atmosphere and entering the blackness of space. At the transition zone between atmosphere, light, and blue sky and the darkness of outer space, there is nothing to hinder our passage other than the decreasing light. There is no "vault" or "firmament," no beaten-out metal barrier to mark the transition. There is nothing out there to protect us from the "abyss" (*tehom*). There is no need for such protection from the primeval waters because, for us, there are no primeval waters.

For those who first heard Genesis 1, the opposite was the case. The word "vault" (*raqia'*) was prominent in the Creation account because it had to be. Without it there was nothing to protect the "land" (*'eretz*) from the threatening waters of chaos. The Genesis account began with the creation of the "vault" by necessity. The first audience could picture "sky" and "land" and "all that in them is" only if a protecting vault was there first. Without it there was nothing to hold the waters of chaos at bay.

The fact that no one in today's world brings "vault" to mind when thinking about Creation goes a long way toward explaining why science and religion have been at odds for the past 350 years. When, in the time of Galileo, more and more people realized that Earth was not the center of the universe, it was not only the position of humanity that suffered from that demotion; in a significant sense the "vault" suffered even more.

During and after Galileo's conflict with the Inquisition, Earth's position was lowered from the center of everything to that of the third planet out, orbiting around a sun in the outer reaches of one of the spiral arms of the Milky Way galaxy. The vault (or "firmament") endured an even more ignominious fate. To the author and audience of Genesis 1 it played a pivotal role in the narrative of Creation; it held a position so important that without it, Creation as such could not continue. From that position of preeminence, it fell into an obscurity so profound that if we think of it at all, we think of it with embarrassment.

Really *hearing* Genesis requires us to overcome that embarrassment, to look the vault squarely in the face, to feel its importance in our bones—if we are to succeed in reentering the Genesis world, a world where God was of supreme importance but the vault was to play a critical role in the transformation from the initial state of chaos into a context for human consciousness, morality, and worship.

IMPORTANCE OF THE VAULT

But, one may object, the fact that the narrative of Creation uses the word "vault" (*raqia'*) so frequently may not mean that it was so important; its frequency might simply be happenstance, or perhaps there was some poetic justification.

The "simple happenstance" suggestion is easily disposed of. All who thoughtfully read or hear the Genesis text today recognize its carefully artistic structure. And all agree that the continual references to God—"God said," "God made," "God saw," etc.—were no accident. The same logic applies to the one created reality that is most frequently mentioned in the account of the first three Creation days.

The second objection—that perhaps "vault" is repeated for the sake of poetic impact—can be dismissed with equal facility. It is true that the Hebrew poetry in the Bible often takes the form of repetition, but it is repetition of the same idea in different words—the well-known Biblical phenomenon of parallelism. We refer again to Psalm 19:1 (this time in our own translation) as a convenient example:

"The sky (*shamayim*) tells God's glory,
and the vault (*raqia'*) proclaims his handiwork."

Here "sky" and "tells" in the first line of the couplet are paralleled by "vault" and "proclaims" in the second. Here the poetic impact is obvious. This is not, however, what is going on in Genesis 1, where the sonorous, almost liturgical language describes the function of the vault according to the intention of the Creator. "God made the vault and separated the water under the vault from the water above the vault" sounds like a straight-forward narrative description—about as close as a three-thousand-year-old text could come to "science." But of course it is not science either—at least not science as we understand the term today (about which we will say more later).

In introducing the "vault," the author of Genesis 1 empha-sized by reiteration the fact that it served a vitally important function—"separat[ing] the water(s)." In order to serve this function the "vault" had to have some substance, some solidity, some heft to it. As we explained in chapter 2, the word for "vault," *raqia'*, came from a Hebrew verb *rq'*, which referred to beating a metal ingot into a thin sheet. For the author and his audience, a metal *raqia'*, with its associated solidity, served ad-mirably to protect them and their world from the watery chaos out beyond. It was a chaos that had been mastered by God and was kept in its place.

Centuries later, in a vision of God's throne, the prophet Ezekiel placed that throne above a "vault" made of material that he describes as crystalline (Ezek. 1:22, 23, 26):

> Over the heads of the living creatures there was something like a dome, shining like crystal, spread out above their heads. Under the dome their wings were stretched out straight, one towards another. . . .
>
> And above the dome over their heads there was some-thing like a throne, in appearance like sapphire; and seated above the likeness of a throne was something that seemed like a human form.

And that is how *raqia'*, the dome or vault, was viewed throughout the Hebrew Bible.

A quite different and remarkably modern picture of the

world was expressed by some Greek thinkers, who envisioned the earth as spherical, rotating on its axis, and orbiting around the sun.[4]

- In the fifth century BCE, some Pythagoreans suggested that the earth moved.
- In the fourth century, Heraclides thought that the apparent movement of the heavens was the result of the earth's rotation on its axis.
- In the early third century, Aristarchus hypothesized that the earth and the planets revolved around the stationary sun.
- In the early second century, Eratosthenes calculated the circumference of the earth.

But these ideas eventually lost out to the common-sense view that the earth was stationary and it was the heavens that moved. As late as the fourteenth century CE, the sun and the moon were regarded as set in and carried around the earth by the revolving vault. Here is Martin Luther commenting on Copernicus in 1533:

> "People give ear to an upstart astrologer who strove to show that the earth revolves, not the heaven or the firmament, the sun and the moon. . . . This fool wishes to reverse the entire science of astronomy; but Sacred Scripture tells us that Josue [Joshua] commanded the sun to stand still, and not the earth."[5]

---

4. See Richard Tarnas, *The Passion of the Western Mind: Understanding the Ideas That Have Shaped Our World View* (New York: Ballantine, 1991), 64, 65, 79, 80; George Johnson, "Here They Are, Science's 10 Most Beautiful Experiments," *New York Times,* Sept. 24, 2002. http://www.nytimes.com/ 2002/09/24/science/here-they-are-science-s-10-most-beautiful-experiments.html.
5. Martin Luther, *Tischreden,* 22:2260; quoted in Jerome J. Langford,

Luther's belittling remarks may be partly due to the fact that Copernicus remained a loyal Catholic to his death. In any event, eight years later Philip Melanchthon wrote,

> The eyes are witness that the heavens revolve in the space of twenty-four hours. But certain men . . . have concluded that the earth moves. . . . Now it is a want of honesty and decency to assert such notions publicly, and the example is pernicious.[6]

We have seen how important a role the "vault" played in Genesis 1. We have noted that if we modern listeners to this ancient account actually *hear* the word *vault* in the text, we react with puzzlement or embarrassment. Others, however, have not been content to allow the idea of the "vault" to lapse into obscurity and disappear from the sum total of concepts human beings use and have used to explain reality. Some translators of Genesis 1 have changed the meaning of *raqia'* entirely to make it fit comfortably into modern cosmology. But in so doing, they have distorted the meaning of the text and obscured how important the concept of "vault" was to the author and first audience of Genesis 1.

Beginning in the mid-nineteenth century (YLT), however, *raqia'* has sometimes been translated as "expanse." The possibility for this translation comes from the association between the "beating out" of metal and the consequent expansion in surface area that results. Gold leaf represents a vast increase in surface area over a gold ingot, and a bronze bowl has a surface that is very greatly expanded in comparison to the ingot with which the artisan started. But to move, as some translators do, from

Galileo, Science, and the Church, 3rd ed. (Ann Arbor: University of Michigan Press, 1992), 35.
6. Philip Melanchthon, "Initia doctrinae physicae," *Corpus Reformatorum*, 13:216, 217.

this sense of an expanded metal sheet into "expanse" as a translation of *raqia'* is unwarranted. This has been recognized by the majority of Bible translators. Three recent translations, however, fail in this regard—NIV, NET, and JPS (perhaps most unexpectedly). In fact, NET surprisingly claims, "The Hebrew word refers to an expanse of air pressure between the surface of the sea and the clouds, separating water below from water above."[7]

To translate *raqia'* in this way is as untenable scientifically as it is linguistically. Those who produced these translations evidently are, like the rest of us, uncomfortable with the obvious meaning of the Hebrew word, given its derivation from *raqa'*, "to beat out [metal]." They render *raqia'* as "expanse" because that easily connotes "atmospheric expanse," and "atmosphere" certainly does have a place in our twenty-first-century worldview. Later, NET translates *raqia'* as "platform" in Ezekiel 1, since an "expanse" would hardly serve as a base for God's throne. But, interestingly, TNIV and NIV 2011, both revisions of NIV, have returned to translating *raqia'* as "vault" rather than "expanse." Even in these translations, which are gender-inclusive to be more compatible with modern sensibilities, the translators could find no textual justification for rendering *raqia'* as "expanse."

That *raqia'* is translated as atmospheric expanse simply indicates that it is not only casual readers of the text who have difficulties with really *hearing* Genesis; translators have their problems too. The word *raqia'* is not used in the sense of atmospheric expanse by any Bible writer unless one counts the birds flying "across the face of the vault of the sky" (Gen. 1:20). Even there, the author's evident intent was to distinguish the part of heaven in which the birds fly from the part in which the sun, moon and stars were set.

Furthermore, a "vault" of metal beaten out into a sheet has

7. Footnote 23 to Gen. 1:6, http://bible.org/netbible/.

the advantage of being much easier to picture mentally than an "expanse." For the concrete Hebrew mind of three millennia ago it was relatively easy to picture a metallic, hemispherical vault that "separated the water under the vault from the water above the vault" (1:7). On the other hand, it is quite likely that those who first heard Genesis did not picture the primeval water as the same as the liquid they used for drinking and bathing. Because the Hebrew mind and the Hebrew language seem to have been less than comfortable with highly abstract ideas, it is likely that they pictured the "vault" not simply as protecting from water as such, but also as holding at bay the forces of chaos. It was these waters of chaos, restrained by God at Creation, that partially broke through again at the time of the Flood (Gen. 6–8). The Flood is described in terms that make it clear that it was, to some extent, a return to the chaotic conditions indicated by the opening verses of Genesis 1.

By the time the narrative reached Genesis 1:8, God had completed the preliminary work of Creation. There was a vault separating the waters of chaos above the vault from the waters below the vault, which were later called by various names such as "the great deep" (Gen. 7:11, *tehom* and "the water under the earth" (Exod. 20:4, *'eretz*). By whatever names they were known, large bodies of water continued for centuries to be sources of great fear for the Hebrews.

"Land" and "sky" are familiar enough terms in the modern world, but as we read them today, our mental pictures of "land" and "sky" are not likely the same as those of the ancient Hebrews. For them the conjunction "sky and land" or "land and sky" included far more than the sky directly over their heads plus the land immediately under their feet; it encompassed everything that existed or could even be envisioned as existing. It was, for them, equivalent to what we would mean by juxtaposing "the earth," "our solar system" "the Milky Way," and "the entire universe beyond." The difference is that for them, all the newly created reality existed within the protecting confines of the "vault."

Such was the importance of *raqia'*.

God said, "Let the waters produce
lots of living creatures,
and birds . . ."
– *Gen. 1:20 (OHV)*

CHAPTER FIVE

BIBLICAL INSPIRATION
COMMUNITY, MESSENGERS, AND CANON

As WE HAVE SEEN, "heaven," "earth," and "firmament" are familiar, traditional Biblical words that, with the help of concepts already present in our minds, evoke mental pictures (except in the case of "firmament," which often does not evoke any very definite picture at all). Unless these concepts that already reside in our minds are pulled into the light of day and examined in the light of the actual Biblical text, we are not going to picture "sky," "land," and "vault." Our pictures are going to be quite different from the pictures the corresponding Hebrew words produced in the minds of the first hearers of Genesis 1. And unexamined, taken-for-granted mental images are extraordinarily powerful.

Equally powerful but (usually) equally unexamined concepts bring the phrase "Biblical inspiration" to life, and they affect the way in which each of us as a Christian believer understands what inspiration is and how it operates. An examination of these concepts and the mental pictures with which they enliven the word *inspiration* is our next task if we are to hear Genesis 1 as the first audience heard it more than three millennia ago.

Quite understandably, Bible readers today often think of inspiration as a process summed up in 2 Timothy 3:16a: "All Scripture is given by inspiration of God" (KJV)—that is, more literally, "All Scripture is God-breathed" (TNIV). But unless their experience or training is unusual, they are likely to envision inspiration operating more or less as follows:

- The original writer was given the words to use in communicating eternal truth ("verbal inspiration"); or, alternatively, the writer was given ideas to express in his own words ("thought inspiration").
- Subsequent editing (if any) of the text took place under the direct influence of the Holy Spirit to ensure that errors did not creep in.
- The Holy Spirit also oversaw the process of transmission, so that a copyist did not add or subtract from the text in front of him (yes, the copyists were almost always male) as he produced a new manuscript. This preservation from error continued through the centuries as each successive generation of manuscripts was produced.
- When the Biblical text has been translated into the vernacular, the Holy Spirit has overseen the process and ensured an accurate translation that has adequately and completely transmitted the message of the original writer to modern readers.

In short, the entire process has been divinely designed and managed, so that the transmitted text is faithful to the original and accurate in every respect, with no ideas added and no ideas deleted.

TRANSMISSION

The last three steps describe the overall process of textual transmission, by which the Bibles we hold in our hands have come to us through the centuries between the actual authors and us. This process deserves examination even before we consider the process by which the text itself came into existence. This is so because translation, the final step in the process, differs in one important respect from all of the steps that precede it. The steps of editing, collating, and copying are no longer available for examination; but the process of translation is still occurring, and we can examine it as it happens today.

Translation is a vital final step for the vast majority of Bible readers, who are not able to read the original Hebrew, Aramaic and Greek. Without a doubt, the Bible is the book that has been most often translated from one language to another. Various parts of the Hebrew Bible were translated into post-classical everyday (Koine) Greek between the third and first centuries BCE. Some of these translations were collected into what became known as the Septuagint, which served as the "sacred writings" or "holy scriptures" of Gentile Christianity (2 Tim. 3:16), and is the source of many of the New Testament's quotations from the Hebrew Bible.

Through the centuries, the process of translation has produced a remarkably diverse and informative array of Biblical versions. Through these modern versions we may now sift, looking for a reading that appeals to us, that addresses our faith questions or, perhaps, that provides evidence in support of an idea that we find attractive and want to explore further (or hang onto and promote).

Although it is surely true that God's Spirit was involved in the process of translation and speaks to human hearts through a variety of Bible versions, ideas of "verbal inspiration" are even less applicable to our English translations than to the original documents.[1] This is easily seen in a close examination of the first two verses of Genesis 1:

- "In the beginning God created the heaven and the earth. And the earth was without form, and void; and darkness was upon the face of the deep. And the Spirit of God moved upon the face of the waters" (KJV).
- "In the beginning when God created the heavens and the earth, the earth was a formless void and darkness covered the face of the deep, while a wind from God swept over the face of the waters" (NRSV).
- "To begin with, God brought into existence the sky and the land. Now [as for] the land, [it] was without form or function, darkness covered the water, and God's Spirit hovered over the surface of the abyss" (OHV; see the concluding section of chapter 1, and chapter 2).

The ideas conveyed and the mental pictures evoked in the minds of listeners by these three translations may turn out to

---

1. The most authoritative Adventist statements on the process of inspiration are by Ellen G. White, "Introduction," in *The Great Controversy Between Christ and Satan* (Mountain View, CA: Pacific Press, 1911), v-xii; and "The Inspiration of the Prophetic Writers," in *Selected Messages* (Washington, DC: Review and Herald, 1958), 1:15–23. The latter source includes the following paragraph (p. 21):

> It is not the words of the Bible that are inspired, but the men that were inspired. Inspiration acts not on the man's words or his expressions but on the man himself, who, under the influence of the Holy Ghost, is imbued with thoughts. But the words receive the impress of the individual mind. The divine mind is diffused. The divine mind and will is combined with the human mind and will; thus the utterances of the man are the word of God.

be quite different—and the decision as to which one is most nearly correct cannot, unfortunately, be made definitively on the basis of the authoritative Hebrew text that has come down to us.[2]

In the process of translation, choices sometimes have to be made without clear-cut, definitive textual evidence. Here we have one example: as we explained in chapter 2, the Hebrew text of Genesis 1 starts with the word *bereshith*, "in [a] beginning," or "beginningly," or, less awkwardly, "initially." There is no definite article corresponding to the English "the". A translator who believes the author is talking about the beginning of *everything* may well add the definite article to the text, and the English reader will see "In *the* beginning" (KJV, NRSV, TNIV, etc.). This decision by the translators will likely bring to the mind of the reader or listener the notion of *ultimate* beginnings—of time, space, matter—indeed, of all reality. But if the translator does not add the definite article that is absent from the Hebrew text, the reader or listener may encounter something like "When God began to create" (JPS, NRSV margin), or (as in OHV), "To begin with, God brought into existence . . ."

Without the presence of the definite article, the reader/listener may well envision an event or process more limited than the beginning of all reality. With that sort of introduction, the text seems to be describing the beginning of our more local and circumscribed reality of sky and land, the same entity that is further described in the next sentence. So these alternative translations are significantly different—and all because one translator decided to add the English "the" to the text, and another decided to leave it out. It is commonly observed that "every translation

---

2. This is known as the Masoretic text, which dates from the seventh to the tenth centuries CE. It is generally (but not entirely) confirmed by the Dead Sea Scrolls and by the Septuagint.

is an interpretation"; and here, before we have come to the end of the first sentence of the Bible, we can see that this is indeed the case.

ORIGINATION

It is also the case that, whatever the translation, every reading (or hearing) of the Biblical text is an interpretation; and the way we hear Genesis is deeply influenced by our expectations of the Biblical text generally, and by the way we conceive of the divine inspiration that is the foundation of the Bible—the inspiration that makes it "Scripture." We have already considered translation to be the final step in the transmission of the inspired text, and we will now look more deeply into its origination. How did Scripture come into existence in the first place? Many scenarios have been proposed by Bible students and theologians. Two quite different views in particular deserve our attention.

One way of viewing the process is that the canon came to us through a direct one-way, three-step sequence: God-to-author-to-writings-to-canon. In this view, the stream of inspired communication flowed directly from God to prophet, with no intervening ripples or eddies. (We use the word *prophet* broadly here to refer not only to Isaiah, Amos, and similar figures, but also to any of the other Bible authors, including historians, poets, and apostles.) The means by which this direct communication occurred has been variously described theologically as "verbal inspiration" or "dictation." Common to explanations of this sort is the belief that the prophet's mental equipment and processes were of minimal or no importance as the message was received from God and transmitted to others.

Subsequently, the God-given and God-controlled communication was written out and the documents were preserved by the community of which the author was a part. Later still, the various preserved documents were collected into the canon, the authoritative criterion of the faith and practice of the community. And that canon, translated into our own language, is what we have today and regard as "Scripture."

GOD
↓
Prophets
↓
Writings
↓
Community Representatives
↓
CANON
↓
Community at Large

The flowchart (above) may help, in spite of the shortcomings inherent in any attempt to encompass a complicated process on a two-dimensional page.

An alternative view to the vertical, directly flowing stream of inspiration diagrammed above sees the process as more like a meandering stream with ripples and eddies—a process in which the prophet's community (and often subsequent communities) played a significant role. According to this view, in addition to God and prophets, inspiration also involved God's people, the community of believers. Indeed, it involved the prophet's community in several ways, and may be summarized as God-to-community-and-prophet, prophet-to-community-to-prophet, prophet-to-writing (or prophet-to-community-to-writing), and eventually writings-to-community-to-canon.

Thus, in this view, over the centuries God communicated with a community of believers. Present in the community were persons who were more than usually sensitive to what God was saying (and doing). They "laughed when God laughed and cried when God cried"; they saw more clearly than most where God was leading the people—in short, they were *prophets*. At times God talked to one of them directly; most often, however, it was out of the interaction between God, the people, and the prophet that the prophet's understanding of God originated, developed, and was subsequently put in writing. The writings that most clearly (as judged by the community) reflected its collective understanding were assembled and preserved by that community and/or subsequent communities, and eventually became the canon. They became "Scripture." If reduced to a paper representation, the process was something like the second flowchart (below).

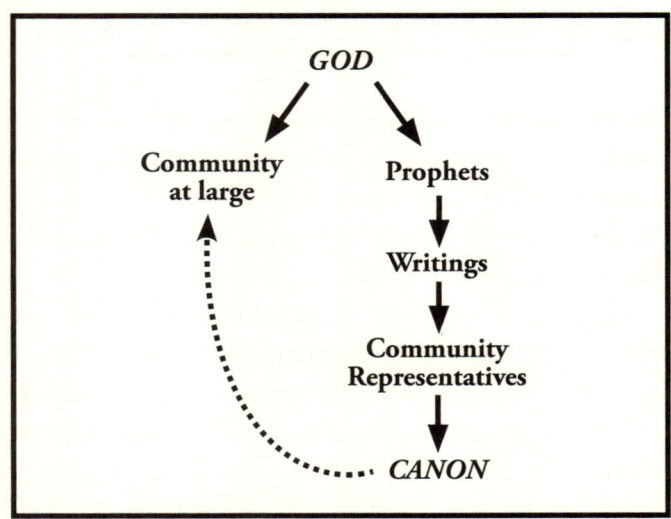

Someone may object that this is all purely theoretical, and that these philosophical/theological musings are of no practical value. But this is by no means the case. These theoretical musings are vital to our task of really *hearing* Genesis 1. In addressing the disconnect between Genesis and science these considerations are more than just important; they lie at the base of the problem itself. It is true, of course, that inspiration may have operated in direct God-to-prophet-to-writing fashion from time to time. The present question, however, is whether Genesis 1 constitutes such an instance. Does the expression "the sky and the land" refer to the "everything that exists" of the author and his community, or does it refer to the universe as it is known by God and (to some very limited extent) by us in the twenty-first century?

Someone who has a settled conviction that the stream of inspiration always flows directly from God to prophet without any ripples and eddies, and that Genesis is to be understood as coming from God-to-prophet-to-writing, may reasonably conclude that Earth is only a few thousand years old and that every living thing and the earth itself came into existence during six consecutive, contiguous twenty-four-hour time periods. Pursuing this line of thought further, this person could appropriately regard the disconnect between Genesis and science as a temporary affair that will, in time, blow over—when more scientific evidence is discovered. So what is required is patience. After all, God told the prophets what to write, God is omniscient, and God surely does not lie.

If, on the other hand, the stream of inspiration is understood as more complicated—as in the "God-to-community-and-prophets" approach—then the findings of science can be taken seriously to the extent they are verified and thus more likely than not to be true. As a consequence there will be a serious and ongoing attempt to incorporate those findings into an understanding of the way things are and how they came to be this way. There will be a recognition that when Genesis was composed, both the prophet (the author) and the community of which he was a very important part pictured a reality that consisted of the sky and the land, and was protected from chaos by a "vault." Furthermore, the "vault" turned one cycle every twenty-four hours and carried with it the "larger light," the "smaller light," and the stars. In short, there will be a recognition that "the sky and the land" of Genesis 1 differs immeasurably from the "universe" of today.

All will agree that "God does not lie." The question here, however, is a very different one—namely, "Did God write Genesis?" A substantial number of Christians would say yes, God did write Genesis; in fact, God dictated it to the prophets, who in turn placed the words on tablets, parchment, vellum, or papyrus. Thus there was only one Author who, in very different times and places, employed various human secretaries.

This, of course, is not the only possible answer to the question of the divine authorship of Genesis. Other Christians would say that while the Bible is indeed the result of divine inspiration, the concepts, the language, and the logic are essentially human. How could it be otherwise? Surely the mind of God cannot be expressed in human language. Divine inspiration illuminates and motivates the prophet, but it does not eliminate the humanness of the prophet. To be human is to be conditioned by one's own intelligence, interests, experience, and information; and one's interests, experience, and information are conditioned by one's cultural context. So, at the same time one says that God was the ultimate *source* of Genesis 1, one can also say that God was not its immediate *writer.*

Almost everyone who has really *listened* to the Bible and has thought seriously about its "inspiration" finds this latter perspective more adequate to the Biblical evidence. The varying literary styles and thought processes make it evident that in the Bible we have not only the result of divine inspiration but also the imprint of a remarkably wide diversity of human minds. We need only to look at (and really *listen* to) the diversity of the Bible's contents. Not only is God not the direct author of the Bible, but the explanatory concepts it contains are not God's own explanatory concepts either.

It is not an expression of presumptuous hubris to recognize that humankind has acquired a great deal of additional information, explanatory concepts, and general understandings of the natural world since Genesis 1 was composed. It is entirely reasonable to suppose that at least some of this additional information and comprehension represents some kind of progress in understanding "how things really are." While it made perfectly good sense for the author of Leviticus to list bats among the unclean birds that were not to be eaten (11:19), it is now well known that bats are mammals, not birds. Similarly, it was entirely appropriate for Matthew's Gospel to represent Jesus as describing the mustard seed as "the smallest of all seeds" (13:32), although botanists know that the orchid seed is actually smaller.[3]

So it is hardly surprising that the concepts we use to explain the origin and operation of the universe differ from the concepts of the audience that first listened to Genesis 1. And because we have had more time, opportunity, and means to explore these things, and have developed means of accumulating vast amounts of information, it is highly likely that our present concepts and understandings of the natural world are nearer the truth.[4] However,

---

3. In an apparent attempt to preserve the notion of verbal inerrancy, NIV (but not TNIV or NIV 2011) reads "the smallest of all your seeds," adding the qualifying word "your" without any textual support whatsoever.
4. See John Polkinghorne, *Faith, Science and Understanding* (New Haven, CT: Yale, 2000), 79: "Scientists are mapmakers of the physical world. . . .

before we sprain our elbows in patting ourselves on the back, we should remember that our information, concepts, and under-standings too are limited, and that there is much, much more to learn. Our present understandings of the universe will almost certainly seem as strange to our successors as the worldview of Genesis 1 seems to us.

What we have in Genesis 1 is not a description of physical reality as we now understand it actually to be, but physical reality insofar as it was understood by the author and his audience.

WHAT WAS THE AUTHOR TALKING ABOUT?

We think of our effort in this book as a retro-translation (and not simply a *re*translation) because we believe that the inspired author was talking about the origin of all the created reality he and his audience knew in terms of the explanatory concepts that were present in their minds. Those who read or listen to this narrative in the Western world of the twenty-first century, however, are almost certainly going to hear it in terms of our modern information and explanatory concepts—and therein lies the problem of really *listening* to Genesis 1.

So what was the author trying to do? What was he talking about? It has been proposed that Genesis 1 is one of the follow-ing:

- A historico-scientific narrative that accurately portrays reality.
- A pre-scientific narrative that is filled with factual error.

In the sense of an increasing verisimilitude, of ever better approximations to the truth of the matter, science offers us a tightening grasp of physical reality."

- An extended poetic metaphor in which the plain sense of the words does not correspond to reality.[5]

Alternatively it is possible to propose a matrix that seems to include all of the relevant possibilities. Given such a matrix, we may proceed to list all of the logically possible combinations: Genesis is a book with both theological and historical/scientific propositions. Therefore the four logically possible conclusions are the following:

- the theology of Genesis is true, but the historical/ scientific elements are false; or
- the theology of Genesis is false, but the historical/ scientific elements are true; or
- the historical/scientific elements are true, and the theology of Genesis is true; or
- the historical/scientific elements are false, and the theology of Genesis is false.

The problem with both of these approaches is that, as lawyers would say, they "assume facts not in evidence." That is, they assume that because the categories of "pre-scientific," "historical/ scientific," and "theological" are present in our minds today, they were also present in the minds of the author of Genesis 1 and his audience. That, however, is manifestly unlikely. And if these categories were not present in their minds, then all of our list-making approaches and matrix-assembling approaches fail. This is a matter of fundamental importance to our task of really *hearing* Genesis, and we will return to it in chapter 6.

Still, the author was unquestionably hoping that his message

---

5. Steven Boyd, quoted in Larry Vardiman, *RATE in Review: Reading Genesis as History*, Acts & Facts 36 (2007), 11:6.

would be heard, understood, and heeded by those who invested the time and effort to listen. We, too, should invest the time and effort to listen, and thence to hear, understand, and heed. Among the things the author of Genesis 1 was trying to do was to explain to his audience how the world they knew came to be—or, as modern philosophers like to say, why there is something rather than nothing—and to assert that the entire process was under God's direction. He may have also been providing (a) an alternative to contemporary Creation narratives that picture gods battling against evil, (b) an explanation of the meaning of the Sabbath, and/or (c) an argument for the superiority of the Hebrew God over the nature gods of the surrounding nations.

In trying to accomplish his tasks, the author had problems that we as his twenty-first-century hearers no longer confront. We think differently about how things come into existence, persist for a time, and then disappear. We manipulate such matters in our minds by calling on the laws of nature, and we draw a clear dividing line between the natural and the supernatural. But these thoughts were not an option for those who first listened to Genesis 1. When there is no natural there can be no supernatural; for the second term has meaning only in contrast to the first. The author did not employ the explanatory concept of miracle either; for when there is no realm of "nature" there are no events that are "miraculous" by failing to be explained by "the laws of nature." As far as the author was concerned, everything his narrative described was the result of God's decision and action, and that was the way his audience understood it. Nothing "just happened"; whatever could not be explained by human action was the result of divine activity.

On reading it three thousand years later, we have additional conceptual options to bring into play. We can think in

terms of natural and supernatural. We can ask whether this or
that event was the result of a miracle—an intervention by God—
or simply the outworking of nature's regularities, or, if we are
thinking in the realm of quantum physics, a matter of chance
with no discernable cause at all. We can speculate on what was
going on in the rest of the rapidly expanding universe at the
time while picturing Earth spinning on its axis and moving in
an orbit around a sun placed in the outer reaches of a galaxy
called the Milky Way. Through no fault of their own, but as a
result of their particular place in human history, the original
hearers of Genesis 1 could not imagine any of these things,
and as a result they heard an account far different from the
one we hear.

The best approach to understanding what the author of
Genesis 1 was doing is to really *listen* to what he says and try as
hard as we can to adopt the mindset of those to whom his account
was initially addressed. Only then will we really *hear* Genesis 1.
For this purpose it will be worthwhile to look more deeply into
the mental furniture of our own minds and the different mental
furniture of theirs. This is the topic to which we turn next.

To begin with, God brought into existence the sky and the land.

– Gen. 1:1 (OHV)

CHAPTER SIX

EXPLANATORY CONCEPTS

"GOD," "HUMAN," "NATURE," "CHANCE"

An enormous earthquake occurred off the west coast of
Sumatra at 00:58:53 Coordinated Universal Time on December
26, 2004. Now known as the Sumatra-Andaman earthquake, it
registered a magnitude between 9.1 and 9.3—the third largest
ever recorded seismographically.[1] Faulting continued for almost
ten minutes. The earthquake was so powerful that it caused the
whole planet to vibrate, triggering secondary earthquakes in
Alaska and generating a massive tsunami with 100-foot waves
that killed almost 230,000 people.

Why did this tragedy occur? Why were there so many deaths?
An observer with a background in geology would immediately
say that the earthquake was caused by a release of elastic strain
energy at a tectonic-plate boundary. Even without this knowledge, most Westerners assume that there are adequate scientific
explanations for the earthquake and the tsunami that followed.

But many others in the world disagree. Within three weeks
after the earthquake and tsunami, a survey was conducted involving

---

1. http://earthquake.usgs.gov/earthquakes/world/historical_mag.php

1,000 people in each of twenty countries.[2] The respondents were asked, "Do you think that the devastation caused by the tsunami was an act of God with religious significance?" In Malaysia 50 percent of the answers were Yes, in the United States 26 percent, in Canada 16 percent, and in the United Kingdom 10 percent. Then the respondents were asked to respond to the statement, "I am much closer to God as a result of the South Asian tsunami." To this follow-up question, in Malaysia 50 percent of the answers were Yes, as before; but in the US only 13 percent, in Canada 8 percent, and in the UK 4 percent.

Why did half of the Malaysian respondents attribute the tsunami to God, while in Western countries a large majority did not?

THE WORLD OF GENESIS 1

Even though they live chronologically in the twenty-first century, those who answered Yes to both questions still deal with the unexplainable as did the author and first audience of Genesis 1. This is a world we need to explore if we are to understand the present disconnect between Genesis 1 (as usually read) and science (as commonly understood). This disconnect did not exist when Genesis 1 was composed and first spoken to an early Hebrew audience, and it did not exist generally among Christians until the scientific revolution that began in the sixteenth century.

---

2. GMI Poll conducted Jan 8–12, 2005. Originally accessed on Dec. 29, 2010, at http://www.gmi-mr.com/about-usnews/archive.php ?p=20050119, but the article is no longer available. The poll is described at http://www.businesswire.com/news/ home/20050119005258/en/ GMIPoll-Americans-South-Asian-Tsunami-Act-God (accessed April 19, 2011).

What causes the disconnect? The usual answer holds modern science responsible. This is a reasonable answer, but it is only a partial one. There is also a profound (and often unnoticed) difference between the conceptual world of Genesis 1 and the world most of us live in now. This is the difference in the way we deal with the *unexplainable.*

"EXPLANACEPTS"

To deal with the unexplainable, all human beings rely on *explanatory concepts.* Because we need to refer to this idea so often in this chapter, we have coined the shortened term *explanacept.*

All of us use explanacepts. When we say about an event, "That's just the way nature works," we are thinking of the event as an ordinary result of the natural order (often called "natural law"); thus we are using the explanacept of *nature.* When we say, "It just happened," we are thinking of an event as "random" or "accidental," meaning that we don't have a clue about its cause; thus we are using the explanacept of *chance.* Sometimes, however, we say, "It was a miracle," meaning that supernatural intervention brought about the event; thus we are using the explanacept of *God.* And, of course, we know that many events are the result of actions by people (ourselves or others), thus using the explanacept of *human.*

When we use the explanacept of *nature,* an event explained by the laws (that is, the observed regularities) of nature shares many characteristics with other "natural" events. When we use the explanacept of *human,* an event caused by one or more human beings shares many characteristics with other humanly caused events. An event explained by divine intervention—a miracle—differs in profound ways from events explained by natural regularity or human agency, but in some ways is similar to other divinely caused events. So if a particular explanacept applies to an event or phenomenon, we already know a great deal about it: we know what sort of event it is and where it fits in our overall scheme of things.

The world of Genesis 1 is strange to us largely because of the difference in explanacepts. In that world, everything in heaven and on earth was explained by personal agency, either human or divine. There were only two explanacepts, so if something was obviously not the result of human action, the only other available explanation was that God caused it. Today, on the other hand, we have the two additional, impersonal explanacepts of *nature* and *chance*. Some events that are clearly not the result of human activity we understand as the result of the regularities of the physical universe. Others we regard as "accidental" or "random" because their exact causes are unknown or incalculable. We may, for example, know theoretically the various physical factors that cause dice to land as they do—weight, momentum, centrifugal force, coefficients of friction, etc.—but because we cannot calculate (much less control) them, we regard the outcome as a matter of "chance." So, strictly speaking, chance is not a "cause" in the way that human beings, God, and nature are "causes," but it is an explanacept—an explanation, a way of categorizing and understanding an event.

These two additional explanacepts have radically changed the way people think about most of what happens in our world. They are not only additional to the two explanacepts of God (divine) and human that were available to the early Hebrews; they have also become our *default* explanacepts—the ways we instinctively interpret puzzling happenings in the physical world. We understand such happenings as the result of *nature* if we can identify, or assume there must be, a relevant natural regularity, or of *chance* if we can't identify such a regularity.[3] Where *they* defaulted to the explanacept of God, *we* default to nature or chance. Because our default explanacepts are different from those of the early Hebrews, we live in a very different conceptual world.

Whether or not a married woman of the early Bible times became pregnant, her family, neighbors, and acquaintances used the explanacept of God to understand and describe her situation: either God had "closed up her womb" (Gen. 20:18; 1 Sam. 1:5, 6) or had "opened her womb" (Gen. 29:31; 30:22). But faced with the same circumstance today, most of us would assume a natural explanation. Even if we suggested to a woman who failed to become pregnant that she and her husband make it a matter of prayer, we would also advise the couple to go to a fertility clinic to find out what (if any) medical help was available. Thus we would utilize an explanacept that was unavailable to the early Hebrews but underlies not only all modern science but also the everyday thinking of most people in the so-called "developed world."

The arrival of the explanacept of *chance* was another "day the universe changed."[4] When the early Hebrews wanted to know God's will, they often found out by "casting lots."[5] This procedure involved stones, pebbles, or pieces of wood or pottery that were thrown, shaken, or tossed on the ground. Because of this practice, the Hebrew word *goral*, "lot," came to mean also "destiny" or "fate "

It was understood that the result of casting lots necessarily

---

3. Whether the "unknowability" of the causality of some events is epistemological, simply reflecting the limitations of human understanding, or is sometimes ontological, inherent in reality itself, is the subject of ongoing discussions in quantum physics and the philosophy of science. Fortunately, the eventual outcome of these discussions is not relevant to our argument here.

4. James Burke, *The Day the Universe Changed* (Boston: Little, Brown, 1985). The book accompanied a television series.

5. See, for example, 1 Sam. 10:17–24; 14:42; Jonah 1:7.

reflected God's will, because there was no other available explanation. In the Wisdom literature, this equation of casting lots
with God's will is explicit: "The lot is cast into the lap, and [or
"but"] the decision is the LORD's alone" (Prov. 16:33). There is
no doubt here about the author's meaning: when lots were cast,
God controlled the outcome. Thus casting lots revealed how
God wanted the land of Canaan to be divided among the tribes
of Israel (Josh. 18:6); and hundreds of years later the disciples
of Jesus cast lots to discover God's choice of an apostle to replace
Judas (Acts 1:23–26).[6]

This practice was similar to one we often associate with
gambling. The last place we today would look for evidence of
God's will for our lives is a roll of dice. How could they have
thought that casting lots gave them access to the mind of God?
Or, on the other hand, how is it that we cannot imagine proceeding as they did? The answer, very simply, is that we understand
reality very differently because we have access to, and utilize, the
explanacept of chance.

When we roll dice, draw straws, or flip a coin (the modern
American forms of casting lots), we are using a process of chance
as a convenient way to ensure that the outcome is beyond human
influence—that it is indeed a matter of *chance*. This method of
deciding a minor question is entirely acceptable to us so long as
no behind-the-scenes manipulation is involved. The early Hebrews
used a similar process for a similar reason: to ensure that the

---

6. For some readers, the selection of Matthias as the twelfth disciple
by means of casting lots may recall the Old Testament account of the
identification of Achan as the guilty person who appropriated for himself
property from the spoils of Jericho (Josh. 7:14–21). Although in this
instance the outcome of the casting of lots was confirmed by a confession
of guilt, this Biblical story is relevant here primarily as another illustration
of the vast difference between ancient Hebrew and modern Western ways
of determining objective truth and the will of God.

outcome was beyond human influence. If they eliminated the explanacept of human, their only alternative was the explanacept of God. When we in similar circumstances eliminate the explanacept of human, the outcome goes to the explanacept of chance.

Because the Hebrews knew only two kinds of causal agents, God (divine) and human, they understood events in terms of only two explanacepts. But the categories were a little more complicated than the language "only two explanacepts" may imply. The explanacept of God included not only everything caused directly by God, but also everything caused by angels and evil spirits—all of which, along with Satan, were understood to be under the ultimate authority of God.[7] The Hebrews eschewed a multiplicity of gods and ascribed everything superhuman, both good and bad, to the one true God, YAHWEH, the LORD. Similarly, the explanacept of human included sub-agents such as animals: a wayward goat or ox might cause mischief or damage. But the major players in the explanacept of "human" were persons.

In the world of Genesis 1, the explanacept of God was easily the dominant one, encompassing everything not clearly attributable to human beings. In our world, however, the domain of the explanacept of God has become for most people much, much smaller; now the explanacept of nature predominates. Almost all physical reality and process has been moved from the explanacept of God to the explanacept of nature. The significance of this massive relocation is enormous—indeed, so enormous that it has been radically misinterpreted by contemporary militant atheists to imply that there is no reality corresponding to the word *God*.

---

7. See 1 Sam. 16:14–16; 1 Kings 22:21–23; Job 1:6–12. This also includes the serpent in the Garden of Eden, which is not explicitly identified as Satan but had a clearly demonic character and role.

The other explanacept that was absent from the minds of those who first heard Genesis 1—chance—has also had a significant expansion. For the early Hebrews, what we think of as chance was also part of the explanacept of God. This was true as well for the surrounding nations, where small images of the gods of chance and fate (such as the Roman goddess Fortuna and the Greek goddess Tyche) were present in many household shrines. People thought that if they reverenced these images, the respective gods would smile on them and accidents would not happen to them. Thus they too incorporated the idea of chance into the explanacept of God. This, however, cannot be the case for most of us who have inherited the thought patterns of the post-medieval world; for most of us most of the time, chance events are not evidences of divine agency, no matter how puzzling they are. Most of us do not actually believe that "nothing happens without a purpose."

How important a role we assign to chance depends largely upon our understanding of the nature and extent of divine action in the world. For those who have no use for God and have ruled out the possibility of divine action, the realm of chance has become the fundamental explanacept, the basic characteristic of reality itself. They believe that all that has ever existed, now exists, or ever will exist is ultimately the result of chance; in their view the universe itself arose from a random fluctuation in the primordial quantum vacuum.

The logic here is perfectly straightforward. That the universe exists is obvious. If the explanacept of God is unavailable, then the reality we experience must be accounted for on some other basis. For those who admit only the explanacepts of human, nature, and chance, the only plausible explanation of reality *as a whole* is chance, because "human" and "nature" are constituent parts of the whole. But at this level—thinking of reality as a whole—for many thoughtful people the idea of chance is profoundly unsatisfactory as an explanation, because what the idea of chance means is that *we have no clue about a cause or purpose.*

EXPLANACEPTS AND GENESIS

The world of Genesis 1 was a world with only two explanacepts. What might it be like for us to have only two explanacepts in our minds, only two file folders in the drawer, only two categories for our understanding of how things happen?

To the extent that we succeed in entering that kind of world, we find it very strange indeed. We have briefly noted the strangeness of a world in which a wife who failed to become pregnant was, just because of that failure, seen as under the displeasure of a God who had "closed up her womb." That strangeness was due to the absence of the explanacept of nature. We have also noted the strangeness of a world in which casting lots was an avenue to the mind of God. This time the strangeness was due to the absence of the category of chance. But this, we repeat, was precisely the world of the author and original audience of Genesis 1.

Most of us today do not (and probably cannot) regard infertility as evidence of God's displeasure, nor do we resort to processes of chance to gain access to the mind of God. This is true even if we are firm believers in the gracious God at the heart of the Christian "good news." There are, of course, exceptions to this generalization. Some of us can subject a heartfelt need for guidance to an apparently random process and act on the result. Thus some Christians open a Bible, close their eyes, point to a verse, open their eyes, read the verse, and believe they have received a divine directive. But this procedure—like the ancient

Roman practice of studying the flight of birds, or the Hebrew custom of casting lots—involves incorporating the explanacept of chance into the explanacept of God. Most of us in the Western world of the twenty-first century do not do this, because we do not believe we can thereby discover God's specific will in a particular situation. That would be like basing a major decision on the flip of a coin.

The early Hebrews did not think about things in exactly the same way we do. They were not less intelligent, and we are not smarter; the difference is that we have far more information about the physical world, and as a result we understand it much differently. To that extent we live in a very different conceptual world.

The difference in explanacepts is our biggest obstacle to re-entering the world of Genesis 1 and hearing its narrative of Creation the same way the original hearers heard it. The author accounted for all known reality in a two-explanacept mode. To the first hearers it was perfectly clear, because it was the mode in which they lived and understood all their experience. We, however, hear Genesis 1 with four-explanacept ears and understanding. Once a mind has been furnished with four explanacepts, returning to a view of reality that utilizes only two—and then to understand reality entirely in those terms—is very difficult indeed. Recognizing this difficulty greatly affects the way we understand Scripture.

"GOD OF THE GAPS"

One other aspect of modern life is significantly affected by the increase in the number of explanacepts from two to four. As we have seen, in a two-explanacept world all the unexplained phenomena of nature were attributed to God. This led to a

"God of the gaps" way of thinking, in which God's actions accounted for aspects of reality that were otherwise unexplainable, and those aspects were therefore regarded as evidence of God's existence. With the addition of the explanacept of nature, however, science provided explanations for more and more of the phenomena that had been previously understood as direct actions of God. As the explanacept of nature expanded, the relevance of—and the need for—the explanacept of God diminished.

This reciprocal process is a major factor not only in the present disconnect between Genesis 1 and science, but also in the rise of philosophical *scientism.* This is the threefold notion that (1) only what science can investigate is truly *real,* (2) only what science can know is true *knowledge,* and (3) only what science can in principle explain is truly *worth explaining.* Scientism—which is a philosophical view not to be confused with the actual practice of science—is the settled conviction that science will eventually (and probably sooner rather than later) make the idea of "God" a quaint, outdated notion and consign it to the dustbin of intellectual history along with alchemy and astrology.

The optimistic kind of scientism believes that eventually all phenomena will be moved out of the explanacept of God and into the explanacept of nature; the pessimistic kind believes that whatever cannot be moved into the explanacept of nature can be fitted into the explanacept of chance. Unfortunately, believers have sometimes contributed to this situation by making unwise claims that God's direct action is the cause of physical phenomena that are still poorly understood or are in some cases already scientifically explainable.

All of this is an aftereffect of increasing the available explanacepts from human-plus-God to human-plus-God-plus-nature-plus-chance. Recognizing this difference in explanacepts profoundly affects the way we understand Scripture.

LITERAL OR FIGURATIVE?

To the question, "Is the description of creation in Genesis 1 literal or figurative?" the most adequate answer is Yes. A more useful question, however, is, "Why is it so hard for us to hear now what the first listeners heard then?" The answer, simply put, is that much of what they heard as literal we hear as figurative (if we actually hear it at all).

As a case in point, let's recall the first material reality that God brought into existence in the second great creative act described in Genesis 1 (the first creative act, the creation of light, having involved energy rather than matter—although there is no reason to suppose that that distinction was made by the either the author or the original audience). This material reality was identified as the *raqia'* (the Hebrew word that has been trans-lated in older English versions as *firmament* and in more recent versions as *dome* or *vault*), as we explained in chapters 2 and 4. The early Hebrews pictured the *raqia'* of Genesis 1 as something like a beaten-out metal plate that separated the waters that were beneath it from the waters that were above it, protecting the nascent creation of land and sea from the waters of chaos. In the *raqia'* were set the sun and the moon on the fourth day, and it carried the heavenly bodies with it as it turned. It had windows, through which torrential rains came. And, like the rest of Genesis 1, it was understood by means of the explana-cept of God.

Because we now hear Genesis 1 with four-explanacept minds and ears, and know that the sun does not revolve around the earth, for us the heavenly bodies are in the explanacept of nature, and we do not require the explanacept of God to understand their motion. What was literal for the first listeners is figurative for us. This change from a literal to a figurative understanding is masked by the fact that we still refer to the sun as "rising" and "setting"—that is, moving around the earth. The *raqia'* itself, however, remains a problem that nothing can mask. The waters beneath it and the waters above it are a problem; God fixing the sun in it is a problem; its "windows" are a problem. The first *material* thing that God created—the *raqia'*, which the first hearers of Genesis 1 understood literally—we today either interpret figuratively or ignore entirely. The *raqia'* as such we usually ignore; its "waters above" and its "windows" we interpret figuratively. In no way can we now understand it literally as it was understood by the first Hebrew audience.

So was Genesis 1 "science"? Well, yes—as close to our category of "science" as the two-explanacept world of Genesis 1 could allow. Science is, after all, an attempt to understand and explain the world around us. Was Genesis 1 "theology"? Yes, as close as the available means of explaining the incomprehensible creative acts of God would allow. Was it understood as a true narrative of how, by the activity of God, everything came into existence? Absolutely; it was that too. It explained the origin of everything, the Originator of everything, and the place of humanity in the grand scheme of everything. It was—and still is—the inspired, true, and essential account of what happened "in the beginning" to produce the reality experienced by the original hearers and by us today. That is why we call it *Genesis*.

God said, "Let there be lights in the
vault of the sky . . ."
– Gen. 1:14 (OHV)

CHAPTER SEVEN

"THE SKY AND THE LAND" VERSUS "THE UNIVERSE"

HOW PERCEIVED REALITY HAS CHANGED THROUGH TIME

A RECENT LETTER to the editor of a magazine for pastors illustrates the importance of conceptual assumptions (such as those we dubbed "explanacepts" in chapter 6). In an article in a previous issue of the magazine, a physicist had referred to Genesis 1 and in response the reader wrote to this effect: "Although I do not understand all the science that the physicist understands, with what science I do know I conclude that there was a mass of our world in existence many years ago and the 6,000-year existence implied by the Biblical record applies to the inhabited world as we now know it."

The letter writer, referring to "a mass of our world in existence many years ago," was apparently picturing a rocky-watery accumulation, a proto-Earth that had been orbiting the sun since the universe began—starting material for God's creative activity that occurred relatively recently. Like the writer of this letter, many modern readers of Genesis 1 picture its account of

Creation as describing a reshaping of this rocky, watery, inchoate mass into our present Earth.[1]

The unexamined assumption the letter-writer shares with many Christians is that the author of Genesis 1, along with his audience, conceived of the universe—and the place of our planet in it—very much as we do today. The unvoiced reasoning behind this idea seems to be as follows:

- Our present (scientific) understanding of the universe is essentially correct and therefore true.
- Since the author of Genesis was divinely inspired, what he wrote must also have been true.
- If it was true, it was scientifically correct.
- Consequently, both accounts of the universe must be saying essentially the same thing, although (of course) in very different language.
- So, regardless of the difference in language, the author and those who first heard his account must have understood the universe pretty much as we do today.

But when the reasoning is laid out in this fashion and examined in the light of the actual text of Genesis 1, it is clearly mistaken. The ancient Hebrew picture of "the land and the sky" and the modern picture of "the universe" are radically different. This realization, however, dawns only after we examine the pictures going through our own minds as we try to *truly listen* to Genesis 1.

---

1. This kind of assumption seems to underlie current versions of the "gap theory" of interpreting Genesis 1—the view that between Gen. 1:1 and 1:2 (or between 1:2 and 1:3) there is an indefinite period of time. This interpretation, for which there is no textual or contextual basis, is evidently motivated by a desire to harmonize Gen. 1 with modern cosmological estimates of the age of the universe.

So why is the vast difference between "the sky and the land" of the ancient Hebrews and "the universe" of the twenty-first century so important? The picture of the "the sky and the land" (including "the vault of the sky" we discussed in chapter 4) was an essential part of the way *the first hearers* understood the message of Genesis 1, and therefore the way *we* picture the author's "sky and land" determines to a large extent how *we* understand the message of Genesis 1. Since we believe that this inspired narrative indeed conveys "the word of God," we want to understand its divine message as completely and accurately as we possibly can.

But the picture of "the sky and the land" in Genesis 1 can cut the other way too. For many Christian readers, if that picture differs from the one held by astronomers, astrophysicists, and cosmologists today, then the author of Genesis 1 was not "telling the truth" and therefore "could not have been inspired." This is another belief that is widely assumed but seldom examined. The assumption here is that the significance of the Bible hangs on this question: Can the Bible be "the word of God" if its authors did not know what we today know (or think we know) about the universe?

Since conceptions of "the world" (all of known physical reality)—that is, the Genesis 1 author's conception and ours—are fundamental to our task of really *hearing* Genesis, it is worth our while to examine the idea of "the universe" with some care.

THE MODERN UNIVERSE

As we noted in chapter 3, we live a post-Hubble existence. We have surveyed the universe through the eye of the space telescope and have been permanently changed by that experience.

Our present concept of "the universe" is a only a few years old, but we can hardly remember, much less describe in detail, our mental image of "the universe" prior to the launching of the Hubble Space Telescope in 1990. Picturing the universe now, we inevitably include one or more Hubble images in the process. By and large, our lives have been enriched by those images, but for our present task—that of really *hearing* Genesis—the Hubble images have turned a task that was already difficult into one that is well-nigh impossible.

For us, the universe consists of a hundred billion galaxies, and the number keeps on growing as the Hubble eye peers deeper and deeper into space. If we take any one of those galaxies and examine it closely, we see burning balls of nuclear energy—suns. These suns are too numerous to count in the outer reaches of each galaxy, and moving toward the galactic center, they fuse together in a blinding swath of light. The number of suns in a typical galaxy is unknown, but it too is probably in excess of a hundred billion. And what might be circling each of those suns? In recent years, as the search for extraterrestrial life continues, we have been increasingly regaled with information about the many planets that are thought to circle these suns—and that may (or may not) be home to life more or less like ours. These are the pictures that we now take for granted, and as a result these images are for us "the universe."

Our galaxy, the Milky Way, is just one of those hundred billion galaxies in the universe. As galaxies go, it is not particularly distinguished. Likewise, in terms of brightness our sun is rather mediocre; it is a second- or third-rate star. But it is *our* sun and therefore, to us, properly special. It is positioned far from the galactic center (fortunately for us) in one of the Milky Way's spiral arms. And, of course, Earth is just the "right" distance from the sun as the third planet out. Any closer and we would be too hot; any farther out and our planet would be too cold. Thanks to Earth's position, its temperature is, like Goldilocks' porridge, "just right."

Viewed from the nearby regions of outer space our planet is blue, swathed in clouds and outlined against the blackness of space. This image has been embedded in human consciousness ever since the first human foot stepped down onto the moon. Most of us probably think of the famous picture of "Earthrise from the Surface of the Moon" as an automatic response when we hear the word *earth*.

That these images come to mind when we think of the universe is unavoidable. We live in a post-Hubble era. And, likewise, when we look up at the night sky we superimpose these post-Hubble mental images on the flickering points of light.

THE DIFFERENT ANCIENT SKY

For the early Hebrews, on the other hand, those flickering points of light were just that—flickering points of light. So Matthew's Gospel can quote Jesus as saying that before the Son of Man returns, "the sun will be darkened, and the moon will not give its light; the stars will fall from heaven, and the powers of heaven will be shaken" (Matt. 24:29). In two passages the book of Revelation uses the imagery of stars falling to earth. Although these passages are highly symbolic, the images that "the stars of the sky fell to the earth as the fig tree drops its winter fruit" (Rev. 6:13) and that the tail of "the great red dragon . . . swept down a third of the stars of heaven and threw them to the earth" (Rev. 12:3, 4) were not unthinkable—as they would be for us in the twenty-first century. This imagery was rhetorically effective precisely because it could be imagined. For us, picturing a series of suns crashing into our small planet is just impossible.

There are other differences too. To us the word *planet* means an orb in space, circling a sun. We forget (if we ever knew) that for the ancient Hebrews, a planet was simply a flickering point of light that attracted attention by moving among the "fixed stars" that form the constellations in the night sky. The planets attracted attention not only because of what they did but also because of what they failed to do. They did not appear rigidly bound in their courses as did the other stars. They did not appear to be turning with the vault of the sky each night.

We find planets and their behavior to be of merely passing interest, if we ever think of them at all. But how interesting they would be if we took it for granted that all of the fixed stars were embedded in the slowly turning blue-black vault that formed the night sky! Any points of light that did not turn with the "vault of the sky" would generate considerable interest and, quite possibly, alarm. Not surprisingly, these strangely acting stars, moving points of light, came to be called "wanderers." (The Greek word was *planetai,* which developed from the verb *plan-asthai,* "to wander," and from which the English *planet* is obviously derived). Since these stars belonged to the realm where the gods dwelt and since the gods alone knew the future, the strange behavior of the planets signified events that would affect human beings. The result was astrology.

For many in ancient times, the planets, along with the constellations of the fixed stars and the moon at night and the sun by day, belonged to the "vault of the sky," the realm of the gods. In this regard, however, the Hebrews differed from their neighbors. The Canaanites, for example, worshipped these objects as gods, making offerings not only to Baal, but also to "the sun, the moon, the constellations, and all the host of the heavens" (2 Kings 23:5)—that is, the whole array in the sky.

For those who first listened to Genesis 1, what they heard did not refer to merely incidental matters; indeed, it contained a new perspective on reality! The sun and the moon, for example, were reduced to timekeepers without specific designations, although the Hebrew language had readily available words for "sun" (*shemesh*) and "moon" (*yarech*); and the stars were mentioned only in passing. "God made two great lights—the larger light to dominate the day; the smaller light to dominate the night—as well as the stars" (1:16). The planets were not mentioned at all.

THE "VAULT OF THE SKY"

It is apparent by now that we have consistently associated the phrase "vault of the sky" with the world of the ancient Hebrews. This has been deliberate. A specific term for the world-reality of the ancient Hebrews is useful because that world differed in so many ways from the "universe" of the present. Because our goal is to *hear what they heard* and to *picture what they pictured,* it is useful to employ a different term from the one that inevitably evokes modern astronomical images in our minds.

For the rest of this book, "vault of the sky" will refer to the whole array dominated by the sun and the moon (Gen. 2:1) according to the ancient Hebrew understanding and picture. Not only was it the home of the gods (including YAHWEH, the Hebrews' own God), but the calendrical information they could obtain from it was critical to human life on the land below. In contrast, the word *universe* will refer to what the term ordinarily means today—including the solar system, the Milky Way, and a hundred billion other galaxies with an average of a hundred billion stars in each. (That amounts to a hundred billion times a hundred billion—

10^{11} x 10^{11}—which is 10^{22}, or 10,000,000,000,000,000,000,000, or ten sextillion stars.) And there may be as many planets as stars.

But there is more to be said about "the vault of the sky." It was not exactly the same for everybody, because the elevation above the horizon of the North Star got higher and higher as the ancients traveled farther north. Going in the opposite direction, the North Star dropped toward the horizon for those who traveled south. And the farther south they went, the more vertical were the tracks of the rest of the stars.

We might suppose that when they observed this change in the orientation of the "vault of the sky" as they journeyed, the ancients should have realized that it was *they* who were moving across the surface of a sphere. For us, with our knowledge of astronomy, that seems an obvious and inescapable conclusion. For them, however, it was simply inconceivable. Had they imagined themselves traveling down the side of a sphere until the star tracks ran vertically overhead, they would have expected all of the water in the seas and lakes to drain out as they got farther and farther down the sphere. But that obviously did not happen. Without an understanding of gravity and its effects on water (and on travelers as well), picturing themselves moving over the surface of a sphere was impossible. For them, it was "the vault of the sky" overhead that moved—the vault to which the sun, moon, and stars were attached.

Eventually, traveling far enough to the south—following the Nile toward its source, for example—they would come to a point where a very strange thing happened. On one or more days in summer a stick placed vertically in the ground would, at midday, cast no shadow at all. Half a millennium later the Greeks (or at least one Greek, Eratosthenes) did figure this out. Before the time of the Greeks, someone established an observatory in the desert on the Nabta Playa, west of present-day Aswan in Upper Egypt.[2] This observatory was located on what we know as the Tropic of Cancer, and at the midsummer solstice people could observe at midday the stick without a shadow.

Such discoveries were, however, still in the future for those who first heard Genesis 1. For them, "everything that is" consisted simply of the disk of land on which they lived and moved and the "vault of the sky" turning majestically above. This picture of the "vault of the sky" survived for a long time after Genesis 1 was first articulated. Indeed, it survived with only minor changes until as late as five hundred years ago, if Martin Luther and Philip Melanchthon[3] were representative of their contemporaries. It was only with the dawn of experimental science and the invention of the telescope that our modern picture of the universe began to take shape.

But even as the first audience listened to Genesis 1, the "vault of the sky" had already been studied for many centuries. We know this to be the case because of observatories like one on the Nabta Playa, the solar temples in South America, and the thousands of neolithic stone circles in the British Isles. The earliest devices for analyzing, predicting, and even utilizing happenings in the "vault of the sky" as a calendar had evidently been in existence for a couple of thousand years before Genesis 1 was written down.

THE ROLE OF EXPLANACEPTS

Before we complete our consideration of the way in which the "vault of the sky" differed from today's cosmic universe, we

---

2. See, for instance, http://sunearthday.nasa.gov/2005/locations/egypt_stone.htm

3. See chapter 4, 73–74.

will explore the vicissitudes of the journey from one to the other, and see how the human understanding of reality changed as a result. It was not simply a removal of the "the sky and the land" from the explanacept of God and their relocation (now renamed the "universe") into the explanacept of nature. As we saw in chapter 6, the journey was more complex.

If the observer is a theist, the origin of today's universe is ascribed to God; but if the observer is a nontheist, its origin—and the origin of everything in it—is ascribed first to chance and after that to nature. This relocation of the explanation of "the sky and the land" from God to nature makes our task of really *hearing* Genesis 1 difficult. The overarching concept that undergirds Genesis 1 is that God is the Source of absolutely all of known reality. The author speaks because he wishes to emphasize—indeed, to declare from the housetops—that God is the one-and-only Creator, that we ourselves are the result of God's creative activity, and that everything that was, is, or ever will be exists because of God.

For those who first heard Genesis 1, God was the Creator of "the sky and the land"—a phrase that encompassed all the things they encountered, knew, or imagined. For us, living three thousand years later, "the universe" includes all the physical reality we have encountered and know about—and God is still the Creator. The fact that the operations aspect of the universe is now viewed as part of "nature" while the origins aspect is still ascribed to God does not change this fundamental "given"; God is still the Creator of the universe. If God is the Creator and the ultimate Source of our own existence, then we owe God our allegiance, our worship, and our service.

When, however, the origin of the universe is moved to the explanacept of "chance," the fundamental message of Genesis 1 is irretrievably lost. If the truth of the matter is that the universe came into existence as the result of a chance fluctuation in a quantum vacuum (whatever that term may mean), and if the universe is maintained in existence solely by regularities of nature that also arose by chance, then for us reality is different indeed: we have no Creator-designed destiny to fulfill, relationships to maintain, or service to perform. What is worse, if our existence is the result of blind chance and mindless nature, our lives have no ultimate significance; and we ourselves are just meaningless replications of the chance fluctuation that brought the universe into being in the first place.

Over against this stark and dismal picture stands the message of Genesis 1. It reassures us that we human beings, along with all the rest of finite reality, are ultimately willed into being by a generous God who extravagantly creates. Our lives have meaning as we serve and fulfill the purpose for which we were created— namely, to enhance the human (and other) reality around us. As a result of our Creation, we have freedom to decide how we will invest our time and our physical, mental, social, and spiritual resources. Fundamental to the message of Genesis 1 is the idea that we are part of a divine Creation, capable of fulfilling (at least to some extent) God's purposes.

While our post-Hubble vision of a universe with ten sextillion suns (and perhaps as many planets) is vastly different from the ancient Hebrew picture of "the sky and the land" and "the vault of the sky," the message of Genesis 1 still fills our hearts and lives with the promise of transcendent meaning.

Now the land was without form or function; darkness covered the water . . .

– Gen. 1:2 (OHV)

CHAPTER EIGHT

"WITHOUT FORM OR FUNCTION"

WHAT EXISTED BEFORE CREATION

IT IS INSTRUCTIVE to read the familiar opening words of Genesis 1 in a translation other than the traditional and well-known KJV. The first two sentences of this translation—"In the beginning God created the heavens and the earth. And the earth was without form and void"—are so familiar that it is difficult for us to actually *hear* them. They slide through our consciousness without making much, if any, impact. This is one of the reasons for our retro-translation: "To begin with, God brought the sky and the land into existence. Now the land was without form or function; darkness covered the water; and God's Spirit hovered over the surface of the abyss."

When we come to the curious Hebrew phrase in verse 2, *tohu wabohu*,[1] "without form, and void" (KJV), most of the recent translations do not help very much. NKJV understandably repeats KJV exactly, "without form, and void"; NIV, TNIV, and NLT have "formless and empty"; NASB has "formless and void"; NRSV has "a formless void." REB does better with "a vast waste,"

---

1. In modern Hebrew this is pronounced *toho vavohu*.

and CEV does better still (though less literally) with "barren, with no form of life."

The expression *tohu wabohu* occurs once again later in the Hebrew Bible, in Jeremiah 4:23, which is a clear allusion to Genesis 1:2. Finally, in Isaiah 34:11 the words *tohu* and *bohu* are included in a parallel construction: "The measuring line of chaos [*tohu*] and the plumb line of desolation [*bohu*]" (NIV, TNIV).

Robert Alter, eager to communicate the literary qualities of the Hebrew Bible—in particular, its emotional, experiential sense—offers the alliterative translation "welter and waste" (RAG). Although the noun *welter* is not now in very common usage (even if it does go back to 1596), its meaning of disorder, chaos, and jumble clearly conveys the meaning of the Hebrew *tohu*. As for *wabohu*, Alter notes that "the second word of the pair looks like a nonce [ad hoc, made-for-the-occasion] term coined to rhyme with the first and to reinforce it, an effect I have tried to approximate in English by alliteration."[2] We have attempted something similar in OHV with "without form or function."

CREATIO EX NIHILO

As theists, we all accept the idea that God the Creator did not need raw materials—elementary matter or energy—with which to undertake the creative process. In Creation God was not dependent on preexisting resources. We believe in *creatio ex nihilo*—creation out of nothing. This makes good sense philosophically and theologically. Our very idea of "God" entails this understanding of creation.

The author of Genesis 1, however, did not make this claim. His account accepted without question that there was something—

2. Alter, 43.

at least water—existing prior to the start of the divine creative activity that the author wanted to describe. What is more, this preexisting water was in some respects a stand-in for "chaos." This water, this chaos, formed the starting condition, the background against which God began the work of Creation.

So there was preexisting matter in Genesis; but was God indebted to it? Not in the sense in which we in the twenty-first century usually ask the question. When we ask such a question, with our scientific mindset, we usually are picturing something material—some *stuff,* some preexisting *matter.* We are asking if God took matter that was amorphous and empty ("without form or function"), and out of it created a perfect pair and placed them in a perfect garden in a perfect world.

A MODERN SCIENTIFIC VIEW

In the last fifty years that hazy picture of *stuff* has become sharper. It is somewhat like the picture in a steamed-up mirror as it slowly clears. For some Christians in the twenty-first century, that preexisting stuff has begun to look more and more like a proto-planet with a core of real rocks, covered with real water, circling the sun. The picture has become more distinct because, despite our best efforts, we cannot keep ourselves from imposing scientific demands on our ancient Creation text—that is, we insist that what the author said *then* make scientific sense *now.*

It is those scientific demands that require a rocky core despite the text's assertion of *tohu wabohu,* "without form or function." The author does, however, describe water—lots of water—as already being here. Of course, there are serious problems with this mental picture. They are typical of the problems that haunt any attempt to impose scientific demands on Genesis 1.

First, the concept of a rocky core covered with water and circling the sun would have been totally foreign to those who first heard Genesis 1. For them, there was no planet Earth in a solar system; there was only "the sky and the land," and the land did not move. It was obviously the sun that moved, being "set" into the vault of the sky. A land that moved was inconceivable. God had providentially established it and placed it firmly on its foundations so that it would never move (Ps. 104:5). God, in fact, was the only one who *could* move it (Job 9:6).

That there were parts of God's created world that did move, the audience (and presumably the author) did not doubt. The sun, the moon, and the stars moved in regular, predictable patterns. A few of the stars, the planets, moved irregularly, in very complicated patterns that could take lifetimes to figure out. The earth, however, did not move. It was the very definition, the example *par excellence,* of stability; otherwise God was not God.

For these reasons the idea of a proto-earth circling the sun was for them quite literally inconceivable. Equally impossible for them to picture was Earth as a planet. As we explained in chapter 7, the term *planet* applied only to certain wandering points of light in the night sky. And that is all they were—wandering points of light in the night sky. They were certainly not spherical bodies hanging in the emptiness of space circling a parent sun, held in their orbits by gravity.

Nor did the ancients have any way of knowing that our sun—the greater light that dominated the day—was of the same nature as those innumerable "fixed" stars that wheeled slowly and majestically overhead each night. That was an idea that, again, was quite literally inconceivable to the first audience of Genesis 1. It was an idea that would remain inconceivable to all humankind for hundreds of years more. Throughout the Bible, including the New Testament, stars could fall to Earth without obliterating it.

There was another complication for the first listeners, a complication that is not apparent to us as we read the text in the twenty-first century. "The earth" (KJV) was for those listeners the land beneath their feet. "Earth" was defined in precisely this fashion in verse 10: "God named the dry ground 'land.' " When God began the process of Creation, dry land was not possible, because there was nothing but water everywhere. Until God created a vault (see chapters 3 and 7) to place limits on this water, *dry* land was not even conceptually possible.

Making *dry* land possible was not the only function of the vault. The vault protected all of creation from the watery chaos that would otherwise overwhelm it. That was its major purpose, and it was a vitally important one.

As for the desire to have radioactive clocks in those rocks ticking away so as to lessen the problem of rocks on earth that appear (by multiple dating methods) to be millions of years old, that idea would have been totally incomprehensible, and not just because an identification of and explanation for the phenomenon of radioactivity was yet three thousand years in the future. To even contemplate such a possibility, we in the twenty-first century have to ignore the author's quite explicit omission from his list of "things present" of anything—any *thing*—other than water and darkness.

And, of course, we must constantly remind ourselves that the author of Genesis 1 was talking about the activity of God, restricting the forces of chaos—the waters—to the realm beyond "the vault of the sky." Within the vault the Creator had the waters "on a leash," so to speak, in a stable environment where plant, animal, and human life could be brought into existence and subsequently flourish.

This environment was described as "land" that was originally "without form or function." This language can show us, as it probably showed its first audience, that the rest of the Creation process rectified, respectively, both the *formlessness* (by creating *formed* entities such as the sky and land and sea) and the *futility* (by assigning *function* to the things that were brought into existence). Thus, an environment that was first described as "without form or function"—an environment that was barely a concept, much less a reality—became by the end of Creation an environment that functioned effectively according to God's purpose.

WHAT WAS THERE BEFORE CREATION

So was something in existence at the time of Genesis 1:2 that could be named "the land," even if it was, at that moment, without either "form" or "function"? Did something—some *thing*—exist before Creation began? This may be a question that we cannot legitimately ask of Genesis 1.

For us, "things" belong to the natural order—the domain of "nature"—and our curiosity about whether the land that was initially "without form or function" actually had a previous physical presence raises a question that assumes that the author and his audience were thinking of entities in the "natural order." But of course they were not, because the idea of a "natural order" was yet thousands of years in the future. The author gave an account of events that resulted from the activity of God. Other than human activity, which obviously was not the cause of these events, God's action was the only kind of activity of which the author and his audience were aware. We cannot properly expect them to understand their reality in any other way.

One thing is certain. At the point of "without form or function" in the Creation account there was no possibility of "land" if it were defined as "*dry* land." There was as yet nothing but water and darkness—the primeval chaos. Yet that is the definition the author explicitly gave his hearers a few sentences later: "God named the dry ground 'land' " (1:10). If we take the text as it reads (and there is no other way we can properly take it) it seems most likely that the author was speaking proleptically about a "land" that later came into existence, indicating already at the point of "without form or function" that the created land—the homeland, the good-earth land, the place where we live, the "land made for you and me"—the land that did not yet exist was soon to be created.

On the other hand, it is certainly possible that the original hearers understood the author as implying that there *was something* there but that it was chaotic, meaningless, and purposeless. A choice between a land that was shortly to be created and a land that despite its futile formlessness had some actual presence may not be all that significant a decision.

Furthermore, an alternative interpretation of the unusual phrase *tohu wabohu* is possible. The ancient Hebrews had a well-known aversion to abstractions. They would, for example, prefer to tell a story than attach a label. So, since the idea of "nothingness" is close to the ultimate abstraction, it might be reasoned that *tohu wabohu* was as close as the Hebrew mind and language could express "nothing."

There may be a clue, however, as to which of the two similar interpretations of the words *tohu wabohu* is more likely. It is the same untranslatable clue we discovered in chapter 8 buried in the subtleties of the Hebrew language. For our purposes here, this particular explanation, "Now [as for] the land," is not to be ignored, for it increases the likelihood that the author was saying that the *dry* land, which at this point in the Creation narrative has not yet appeared, was still without form or function.

The author of Genesis was not beginning a lengthy and

meticulously detailed explanation of the precise material state in which the earth found itself. Rather, he was saying, at this point in the Creation account the land did not consist of anything that would undergird or lead to a proper home for humankind. He appears to have included the "land" along with the "abyss" as part of the preexistent, pre-Creation chaos. At this point the Creator had, so to speak, rolled up his sleeves and, faced with a formless futility everywhere, was about to give "form" and assign "function."

As we noted earlier, the prophet Jeremiah used the same formula, *tohu wabohu*, "without form or function," to describe the state to which the land could well return without God's continued blessing. Without that blessing the land of Israel could return to the condition in which it existed prior to the first act of Creation—the divine declaration, "Let there be light."

We recall that the unusual placement of the Hebrew verb in Genesis 1:2 may have indicated a parenthetical, explanatory function of the sentence. This would support a combination of the first two sentences of Genesis 1 into a single, extended sentence as a build-up to the climactic third sentence: "To begin with, [when] God brought the sky and the land into existence, the land was without form or function, darkness covered the water, God's Spirit hovered over the surface of the abyss. Then God said, 'Let there be light!' "

A CONCLUDING WORD

As we noted near the beginning of this chapter, the second word in the Hebrew pair, *tohu wabohu* ("without form or function")—namely *bohu*, "without function"—has been described as a nonce term (that is, ad hoc, made-for-the occasion) coined to rhyme with *tohu* and to reinforce it. If this is correct, the word has no specific meaning, and any attempt to pin a precise meaning on this artificial word may well miss the point that the author is making—that before God's first act of Creation, the land was *without form or function*, a part of the preexistent, pre-Creation chaos to which God was going to give form and assign function. If this is correct, it is an artificial term invented to rhyme with *tohu*, which means "formless," and to reinforce that meaning. It seems entirely appropriate to understand the text as employing a meaningless word to describe a meaningless condition.

*God said, "Let the land produce
every kind of living creature . . ."*
– Gen. 1:24 (OHV)

CHAPTER NINE

PUTTING SCIENTIFIC DEMANDS ON AN ANCIENT TEXT

FITTING IN 13.7 BILLION YEARS

STEPHEN LANGTON (*ca.* 1150–1228), an English Bible scholar, lecturer at the University of Paris, and later a cardinal and archbishop of Canterbury, is generally credited with dividing the books of the Bible into substantially the scheme of chapters that we use today. Further subdivision into verses came later, so that "the current system is not older than the sixteenth century."[1]

Prior to the development and general acceptance of a standard chapter-and-verse system, it was obviously difficult to identify and locate particular Bible statements. All a preacher or scholar could do was to give a very general reference—something like, "As the apostle Paul says in his second letter to Timothy, 'All Scripture is God-inspired.' " There was no "3:16" to facilitate finding the passage.

The Bible itself reflects this difficulty. Luke's Gospel describes

---

1. *Cambridge History of the Bible.* Vol. 2, *The West from the Fathers to the Reformation,* ed. G. W. H. Lampe (Cambridge, U.K.: Cambridge University Press, 1969), 147–48, n. 6.

an experience of Jesus in the Nazareth synagogue: "The scroll of the prophet Isaiah was given to him. He unrolled the scroll and found the place where it was written: 'The Spirit of the Lord is upon me, because he has anointed me to bring good news to the poor. He has sent me to proclaim release to the captives and recovery of sight to the blind, to let the oppressed go free, to proclaim the year of the Lord's favor' " (Luke 4:17–19).

For all sorts of reasons it is useful to know that the passage was Isaiah 61:1–2a, but this designation didn't exist until fifteen hundred years later. In the book of Acts (also commonly attributed to Luke), the apostle Peter is described as quoting two Psalms that he applied to Judas: "For it is written in the book of Psalms, 'Let his homestead become desolate, and let there be no one to live in it'; and 'Let another take his position of overseer' " (Acts 1:20, quoting Ps. 69:25; 109:8).

These two instances show the value of a system of chapters and verses; but we must remember that they are not part of the oldest (and most nearly original) Biblical *texts*; the chapter divisions come from the thirteenth century and the verse divisions from the sixteenth century. The good news is that we have a commonly accepted system; the bad news is that the system is necessarily somewhat arbitrary.

Occasionally the divisions were unfortunate, and the end of Genesis 1 illustrates one recognized mistake involving chapters and another probable mistake involving verses. There is a strong consensus among modern translators and readers that the Genesis 1 account of creation extends at least three verses into Genesis 2, which provide an account of the establishment of the Sabbath rest on the seventh day. There is widespread agreement that the chapter division here is in the wrong place; Langton concluded chapter 1 several verses too soon.

What is much less clear is the identification of what would

have been the correct place to divide the chapters. In OHV we have placed the division in the middle of what all versions have as verse 4, and have explained the principal reasons for doing so in our chapter 2. Thus we dispute not only the location of the division between Genesis 1 and 2, about which there is general agreement, but also the verse division between Genesis 2:4 and 2:5, about which there is much difference of opinion.[2] We believe that verse 4 should have been divided into two verses, because it contains two different ideas and performs two contrasting functions: it concludes the first Creation account and it opens the second Creation account.

THE CHALLENGE OF GENESIS 1:1–3

At the beginning of Genesis 1 a similar issue has major theological consequences. The issue here is the proper relationship between verses 1, 2, and 3. Does verse 1, for example, "To begin with, God brought the sky and the land into existence," introduce a creative activity that is elaborated in the rest of Genesis 1, or does it affirm a *separate* and *prior* creative activity, earlier (by an indefinite period of time) than the creative activity described in the rest of the chapter?

This is a question that every translator of Genesis 1:1, 2 confronts. There is a period after "earth" in KJV ("In the beginning God created the heavens and the earth."), and after "land" in OHV ("To begin with, God brought into existence the sky and the land."). Thus these translations, separated by 400 years, indicate that the first few words (verse 1) constitute a complete sentence. In contrast, NRSV treats these words as an introduc-

2. Compare, for example, NRSV (1989), NLT (1999), and NET (2005) versus KJV (1611), NIV (1978), NKJV (1982).

tory, dependent clause, ending with a comma: "In the beginning, when God began to create the heavens and the earth, . . ." So the question arises, should the first few Hebrew words be regarded as a complete sentence or as a dependent clause?

This is not a new question; it goes back at least nine centuries to two great Jewish scholars of the Middle Ages—Rashi (1040–1105) and Ibn Ezra (ca. 1089–ca. 1164). Ibn Ezra, like NRSV, understood the first word of Genesis 1, *bereshith*, in relation to verse 2: "To begin with, when God brought the sky and the land into existence, the land was without form or function." Rashi, however, had earlier understood the first word of Genesis 1 as modifying the verb at the beginning of verse 3: "To begin with, when God brought the sky and the land into existence, . . . God said, 'Let there be light.' "[3]

Here, fortunately, the Hebrew text points to a preliminary answer: the first seven words[4] constitute a complete sentence, and the "when" of JPS, NRSV, etc., is an obvious *addition* to the text. There is simply no "when" in the Hebrew original; it is an interpretive insertion, supplied by the translators. In OHV, we have acknowledged the fact that there are, in the first seven Hebrew words, a grammatical subject, verb, and object—in short, a complete sentence. Hence our translation, which is entirely independent of KJV and in many ways stands in contrast to it, also omits the "when."

But we note that the JPS and NRSV translators (along with many others) were not irresponsible or necessarily grinding a theological ax (as has sometimes been the case with Biblical

---

3. See Walter Eichrodt, "In the Beginning: A Contribution to the Interpretation of the First Word of the Bible," in *Creation in the Old Testament,* ed. Bernhard W. Anderson (Philadelphia: Fortress, 1984), 65.
4. Hebrew regularly uses prefixes where English uses separate words; thus "To begin with" translates the one word *bereshith,* and "and the" translates the one word *wᵉha.*

translators). They were responding to two subtle but potentially significant linguistic phenomena.

In the first place, the next Hebrew sentence begins with a conjunctive prefix, *wᵉ*, which is remarkably versatile. Its most common English equivalent is "and," but in various contexts it can also mean "then" (as in the OHV designation of the first six Creations days, "there was evening, then dawning") or "so" (introducing a result) or "now" (in a nontemporal, clarifying sense) or even "but" (introducing a contrast). Sometimes the *wᵉ* means practically nothing at all except that the following sentence is closely related to the preceding one; hence it is sometimes left untranslated. So the translators must make an interpretive judgment about the logical relationship between the two sentences and therefore the function of the prefix that begins the second one. In this case the NRSV translators interpreted the first sentence (about God creating) as giving the reason for the second sentence (about the condition of the existing reality).

A common function of the prefix *wᵉ* at the beginning of a sentence is to indicate an elaboration of a subject recently mentioned. Our view is that here at the beginning of Genesis 1:2 the author meant something like "Now as for the land, it was without form or function." But to avoid adding to the translation several words not in the Hebrew text (and thus veering off the translation track and into paraphrase) we have simply translated the Hebrew as "Now the land was without form or function," believing that in the absence of other evidence, the most natural reading of "the earth" in verse 2 is that it refers to "the earth" in verse 1. Thus we agree that the JPS and NRSV addition of "when" is linguistically justifiable even though we believe it unnecessary.

In the second place, there is another clue that the OHV translation is more likely. Like the first clue, having to do with the meaning of the conjunction *wᵉ*, this one is also buried (and even more deeply) in the subtleties of the Hebrew text. It is a subtlety that is virtually impossible to translate directly into idiomatic English, and so a direct translation is rarely attempted.

A Hebrew sentence, unlike its English counterpart, is normally constructed with the verb preceding the subject. Thus the first sentence in Genesis 1 reads "*bereshith* ["To begin with"] *bara'* ["created"] *'elohim* ["God"]. . . ." The next sentence, however, is put together differently, with the subject preceding the verb (as is usually the case in English). Where this construction occurs elsewhere in the Hebrew Bible, this movement of the subject forward in the sentence usually means that the sentence that begins this way is either an especially important one (the author has done this for emphasis) or that it is a parenthetical explanation of the previous sentence (as seems to be the case here). If that was indeed the reason why the unusual Hebrew construction was employed here, then the original audiences of Genesis 1 heard the author saying something like, "Now [as for] the land, [at this beginning point in the Creation process, it] was without form or function."

We can perhaps appreciate the difficulty of translating a sentence of this type. Communicating the subtleties of the Hebrew verb placement has required the addition of two new phrases composed of a series of additional English words. But, unlike a paraphrase, a translation is assumed to have added no words that were not present in actual language of the original text. So what is the translator to do? Most, at this point in the text, have simply ignored the subtleties of the Hebrew and translated into English only the face value of each of the Hebrew words. For our purposes, however, this particular explanatory, "Now [as for] the land," is not to be ignored, for it increases the likelihood that the author was really describing the problem—the chaos that was "without form or function"—for which the process of Creation was the divine solution.

WHY IT MATTERS

But why does the little Hebrew prefix *w* warrant all this attention? Because the issue here is the relation of Genesis 1:1 to the rest of the Creation narrative (1:2–2:4a) that it introduces. Does Genesis 1:1 affirm one Creation activity, and 1:2–2:4a another, separate activity? That is (to use the distinction made in chapter 5), does 1:1 refer to the ultimate, primordial Creation of the universe, while 1:2–2:4a refers to another, later and more limited Creation of planet Earth (or some aspect of it)? Or does Genesis 1:1 function as a topic sentence, for which 1:2 begins an elaboration, so that only one Creation process is being affirmed and described?

This exegetical issue has significant theological consequences. If the author of Genesis 1 had two different and separate Creation processes in mind, the listener/reader could plausibly insert a period of time—perhaps millions or billions of years—between the initial Creation of matter and energy, and the later Creation of life on planet Earth. In the twentieth century this was for a time a popular way of harmonizing Genesis with science; it was sometimes identified as "the gap theory" (often disparagingly by its detractors). In one form or another this view still has proponents in the twenty-first century, and is essential to a related view known as the "ruin and restoration" theory mentioned in chapter 2. While this two-Creations view cannot be ruled out completely, it is an unlikely interpretation of the Hebrew text that has been transmitted to us.

In the first place, in Genesis 1 there is no indication whatever of two separate Creation processes. On the contrary, the six-day narrative explicitly includes astronomical objects—the "greater light," the "lesser light," *and the stars*—on the fourth Creation day (Gen. 1:16). Furthermore, the description of the

Creation Sabbath that concludes the account specifically states that "the sky and the land were completed, *with all their vast array*" (Gen. 2:1, emphasis added). And the reference to Creation in the fourth commandment says that "in six days the LORD made heaven and earth"—that is, sky (*shamayim*) and land (*'eretz)*— "and all that is in them" (Exod. 20:11). These passages confirm that the most natural reading of Genesis 1:1 is to regard it as introducing the Creation activity that is explained in more detail by the following narrative.

In the second place, Genesis 2:4a, "These are the origins of the sky and the land when they were brought into existence," is clearly an echo of Genesis 1:1, "To begin with, God brought into existence the sky and the land." Sharing the terms "bring into existence" (*bara'*), "sky" (*shamayim*), and "land" (*'eretz*), the two verses function as rhetorical bookends for the account of Creation.

As we explained, the first seven Hebrew words constitute a grammatically complete sentence that can stand entirely on its own. Also, as we noted, the Hebrew conjunction *uͤ* that begins verse 2 often indicates a close logical or narrative relationship between two sentences, so that translating verse 1 as introductory is an entirely reasonable, although not absolutely mandatory, interpretation of the Hebrew text.

THE QUESTION OF 13.7 BILLION YEARS

Even if, as we have just argued, modern readers of Genesis 1 should regard it as a single narrative elaborating a topic sentence, we need to take into account a tendency on the part of some readers and interpreters to insert a period of as much as 13.7 billion years between verses 1 and 2. Specifically, we need to ask whether a major chronological separation between the two verses properly reflects the way in which Genesis 1 was originally expressed and understood. Our question at this point is twofold: (a) Should there be a major separation between the first two sentences of Genesis 1? (b) Does it really matter? The respective answers are: (a) as we noted in chapter 5, we cannot come to a conclusive decision on the basis of the Hebrew words and grammar alone; and (b) yes, it matters a great deal.

Since we have already considered the relevant linguistic evidence, we will now proceed in a different direction—namely, to ask what theological or other considerations might motivate a modern reader or interpreter toward one choice or another.

If those who first listened to Genesis 1 heard a long pause after the words, "To begin with, God brought the sky and the land into existence," then it is possible—though for the textual reasons already mentioned, not very likely—to imagine a period of time after verse 1 and before the account of another Creation, described beginning with verse 2. But why might a modern interpreter want to suppose and suggest this? Perhaps because of a desire to harmonize Genesis 1 as a whole (1:1–2:4) with the current scientific understanding that the universe itself is very old—indeed, 13.7 billion years old—without having to accept the current scientific understanding of the development of life on Earth.

Perhaps some assume (even unconsciously) that the inspired author of Genesis 1 must have known this scientific fact about the age of the universe—and the related fact that the physical matter of which Earth is composed is relatively old, something more than four billion years. But there is no textual evidence whatsoever that he had this kind of information. And if he did understand that the universe was indeed very old, then as he described God's activity in Creation, he had an excellent opportunity to enlighten his listeners. At the beginning of the

Creation account, as the curtain lifted on a scene of darkness, water, and God's spirit, he had an opportunity to indicate to his audience that the earth had existed for eons in an unformed state, after which God was about to begin a reshaping process to make it into a suitable habitat for humanity.

If the first listeners detected a significant pause between the first two sentences of Genesis 1, someone might reason, we should pause there too. We should follow the same sequence: opening sentence, pause, second sentence—with a remarkable parsimony of words covering the vast stretch of time since the beginning of the universe 13.7 billion years ago (or at least since the beginning of planet Earth more than 4 billion years ago).

So is today's reader of Genesis 1 justified in pausing after the first sentence? Our "believer's bias" might encourage us to do so. This bias afflicts all of us who live in the twenty-first century and read with a mixture of awe and enjoyment a Biblical text that is more than three millenniums old. This bias explains our tendency to place unrealistic scientific demands on an ancient text whose author had nothing of the sort in mind.

This also explains why the emotions involved in interpretations of Genesis 1 so often run high. We want the ancient text to be "scientifically accurate" without realizing what we are asking for. What is more, we want it to accord with the science of our own era, not with the science of fifty years or five hundred years or three thousand years ago. If the text is talking about cosmology, we want it to reflect *our* cosmology.

Is it possible for us, residents of the twenty-first century, *not* to place scientific demands on Genesis? Discouragingly, it is highly unlikely, although theoretically possible. That is because we assume that we know what Genesis 1 is, what category it belongs to. After all, it talks about the origin of the sky and the land, and the sun, the moon and the stars. Any such narrative implies a kind of cosmology. An account of how (in some sense) the cosmos and its contents came to be indicates something about them that may be very important to our understanding of them.

Ordinarily we have only one explanacept for such accounts—the explanacept of nature, where everything happens according to natural regularities. Science is the tool we utilize to explore nature; hence it is the tool we automatically apply to Genesis. To do anything else, given our twenty-first-century explanacepts, is at least difficult and almost inconceivable. So we typically do place unrealistic scientific demands on an ancient text whose authors had no such thing in mind. Most of the time we cannot do anything else because we do not think about Genesis in any other terms. This is why many serious Christians say things like "I don't *interpret* the text; I just *read* it," and, "Our faith controls our science; our science does not control our faith." Those who say (or even think) these things fail to realize that every reading *is* an interpretation, and that their own interpretation is that of a modern, scientific mind whose understanding of science inevitably *influences* (although it need not *control*) its understanding of faith.

WHAT THE AUTHOR WAS DOING

If the author of Genesis was not talking science in his description of how the sun, moon and stars were brought into existence, what was he doing? He was doing something that has become well-nigh impossible for us: he was describing the activity of God on the basis of what he saw through the only lenses available to him, and making no attempt to separate science from miracle or theology. He was making no attempt to distinguish between these conceptual categories because they did not yet exist.

For us, obviously, these categories do exist, and we all too easily assume that they must have always existed in the human mind. In making this assumption, however, we inevitably place scientific demands on an ancient text. We suppose that the author formulated Genesis 1 according to our own familiar categories. We expect that, at a minimum, he thought of reality in terms of nature, miracle, and theology; and since he did not do the job, we try unconsciously to do it for him. When our categories cause problems, we blame the Bible, or science, or both. We are not malicious, and we are not obstinate. When we encounter a passage that talks about matters cosmological, biological, chemical, physical etc., we simply cannot deal with it without unwittingly imposing scientific demands on it.

Hearing the text three thousand years later, we want the text to describe the beginning of our universe. In more technical language, we want it to be a cosmogony. But to expect that, in telling of God's creation of "the sky and the land," Genesis 1 is describing how our twenty-first-century universe came to be what we now believe it to be is clearly to place an unrealistic scientific demand on the ancient text. It is to ask a question that in principle cannot logically be asked, because the ancient listeners' realm of "the sky and the land" and our universe are far from coextensive, much less identical. Furthermore, no human language (or ideas) could possibly capture the activity of God.

So what mental concepts may we properly retain as we read Genesis 1? What pictures in our mind's eye will be true to those that were the common property of the writer of Genesis and those who first heard the account of beginnings?

In the realm of cosmology their concepts were gleaned from visual astronomy—from the "vault of the sky" as it turned overhead. And, we should remind ourselves, they observed the scene with only the *unaided* eye. If we are to listen to Genesis 1 accurately we must listen with that ancient picture in our minds too. We must eliminate everything that human beings have learned about cosmic time and space in the last three thousand years. Only in this way can we prevent ourselves from subjecting that ancient text to unrealistic scientific demands.

WHAT GENESIS 1 SAYS TO US

What, then, does Genesis 1 offer to twenty-first-century believers if it is not a handbook of scientific cosmogony or cosmology?

Well, in the first place, Genesis 1 is *worship*. It is a hymn praising the Creator for the mind-boggling reality that the author saw all around him, and saw with his own eyes. It is a hymn to the Creator of all reality (which has become for us far larger [with galaxies, etc.], smaller [quarks, etc.] and more complicated [butterfly effect, etc.] than the author and his original hearers could possibly have imagined).

In the second place, Genesis 1 is, strictly speaking, *theology*—thinking and talking about God (which is what the word *theology* literally means: Gr. *theos* and *logos*). It is primarily *an account of the activity of God*. As even a cursory reading of the text demonstrates, God is the grammatical and logical subject of most of the sentences: "God brought . . . into existence," "God said," "God made," "God saw," "God named," "God completed . . . and . . . rested," "God blessed." The hymn ends with an account of God's own celebration of the entire process (2:1–4a). Thus Genesis 1 confirms for all time that one God is responsible for everything that exists—including energy, matter, life, and consciousness.

In the third place, Genesis 1 is a kind of *theological anthropology.* God's crowning act is the creation of male and female humanity in and as the very image of God—the created reality that is closest to the Creator's own reality, and is responsible for the governance of all the forms of created life. Thus Genesis 1 also confirms for all time that humanity is here as a result of divine generosity and creative love and that the purpose and function of humanity is the ongoing actualization of God's love in a proper stewardship of God's world.

Because there is a single Source of all reality rather than a multiplicity of sources, it is reasonable for us to suppose that reality is fundamentally and ultimately coherent—that in spite of its unimaginable size and enormous complexity, in principle it can all make sense. So a comprehensive view of reality is a rational objective. A scientific, philosophical, and theological cosmology is a plausible (although distant) goal of human understanding.

The reality to which humanity belongs, and of which it is the intended capstone, is a product of divine generosity, not competition or chance. Thus it is essentially meaningful and good, and not in conflict either with the Creator or with other created reality.

And to be human is to have a vocation that is akin to that of creative Deity itself. Brought into existence "in God's own image," humanity has a function that is similarly Godlike—to "be fruitful and multiply," to "till and tame all the land," to "take charge" of the other kinds of life. This is an invitation to ongoing adventure in fulfillment of a mission designed, initiated, and shared by the Creator.

While in one sense humanity is part of physical nature, and its physicality belongs to the goodness of nature, in another sense humanity transcends the rest of nature. Humanity can indefinitely explore, significantly understand, and partially shape its environment and its relationships to the rest of created reality. Its likeness to the Creator is its unique potentiality to engage in a kind of "co-creation." At the same time, humanity never becomes deity; the infinite qualitative distinction[5] between the Creator and the created remains. Even as co-creator, humanity is always created, and its creativity is always derived. Like the rest of created reality, humanity is real (not illusory) and good (not intrinsically evil); but it is also fundamentally dependent (not self-existent).[6]

5. The concept of "infinite qualitative distinction" is often attributed to the Danish philosopher Søren Kierkegaard (1813–1855).
6. See Langdon B. Gilkey, *Maker of Heaven and Earth: A Study of the Christian Doctrine of Creation* (New York: Doubleday/Anchor, 1959).

*God observed everything that he
had made and saw that indeed it
functioned very well.*

– Gen. 1:25 (OHV)

CHAPTER TEN

THE SIX CREATION DAYS
A PROLOGUE TO GOD'S REST

THE FOREWORD to this book began with a quotation that now, at our final chapter which emphasizes the centrality of the "six days," deserves repeating:

> *For almost two thousand years Christians have pored over the biblical texts in an earnest effort to understand them. The greatest minds of the church have spent themselves in this consecrated endeavor. Not least among their concerns has been what the Bible teaches about creation. For this they turned especially to Genesis 1:1–2:3, and studies of the ["six days"] loom large among the writings they have left us.*[1]

What exactly were the six Creation days of Genesis 1? If we try to hear the text as nearly as possible as did those who first heard its magnificent message, can we hear what they heard? This is a point at which the theology/science dialog has boiled over repeatedly ever since Copernicus published *On the Revolutions of the Heavenly Spheres,* in which he moved Earth out of the center of the universe.

---

1. John H. Stek, "What Says the Scripture?" in *Portraits of Creation*, 205.

Where the author used a particular term, we should look first at the rest of the Genesis 1 explanation of Creation to see if the author considered the term important enough to indicate what he meant. Unless we are careful to find and utilize (and thus limit ourselves to) the meanings the author provided (when he did), we will inevitably superimpose *our* meanings upon *his* explanation. This will almost certainly burden the ancient theological explanation with modern scientific demands and all the myriad problems that inevitably follow. The author explained what he intended his hearers to picture when he used such terms as "heaven" (Hebrew *shamayim*, "sky," 1:8) and "earth" (*'eretz*, "land," 1:10). Did he do the same for the "Creation days"?

As we noted in chapter 2, the Hebrew word for day is *yom*, "the fifth most frequent noun in the OT" and "by far the most common expression of time."[2] It had much the same broad semantic range as the present English word *day*. As a general expression of time, the author's use of *yom* could have carried any of the following meanings:

1. Daytime. "God named the light *day*" (Gen. 1:5). This was the predominant meaning of the word *yom* in Genesis and elsewhere. In the semidesert context where the first listeners to Genesis 1 lived, it also meant the warm hours: Abraham "sat at the entrance of his tent in the heat of the day" (18:1); by contrast, God walked in the Garden of Eden "in the cool of the day" (3:8, NIV). The *day* was the time in which work was done, projects accomplished, results achieved. If some activity, condition, or situation continued beyond daytime, that fact was specified, for the "day" had been exceeded. This was the case in the Flood narrative, when it rained "forty days and forty nights" (7:12).

2. An indefinite period of time, essentially equivalent to one of the common modern uses of "when." This is the usage in Gen.

---

2. M. Saebø, "*yom*, II," in *Theological Dictionary of the Old Testament*, 6:13.

2:4 that might, with equal clarity, read, "When God made *eretz* and *shemayim*" instead of "In the day God made *eretz* and *shemayim*," and a few verses later, "When you eat from it you will die" rather than "in the day you eat from it you will die" (Genesis 2:17).

3. A general reference to time (usually plural): "You will eat dust all the days of your life" (3:14, NIV, TNIV); "all the days that Adam lived were nine hundred thirty years" (5:5).

4. A solar day, equivalent to our modern period of twenty-four hours. In Genesis 1, apart from the meaning of the Creation day (which is the question at issue here), this might have been the meaning in relation to the chronometric function of the two celestial lights: "for seasons and for days and years" (1:14). Even here, however, the word probably evoked mental images of work and workdays rather than 1/365 of a year. Elsewhere in Genesis 1 the reference is clearly to daytime: God named the light *day* (1:5); the celestial lights distinguished the day from the night (1:14); the larger and smaller lights were intended respectively to dominate the day and the night (1:16, 18).

So did the author of Genesis 1 use *yom* in a way that enables us to identify the precise meaning he intended? He did. He indicated that he was about to describe the archetypical, paradigmatic Creation day—the *yom* that was to define the subsequent Creation days—but he did so in a way that is not apparent in most English translations (KJV, TEV, NIV, NRSV, etc.). The numbers designating each of the six Creation days have usually been translated as "first," "second," "third," etc. The author, however, designated the first Creation day as "day one" or "one day" (*yom 'echad*, 1:5), using a cardinal numeral ("one," "two," "three," etc.) rather than an ordinal numeral ("first," "second," "third, etc."). In so doing, he set up the archetypical Creation day, beginning with "evening," "darkness," "dusk" (*'ereb*) and proceeding to "dawning," "sunrise," "morning" (*boqer*).

In the narrative explanation of Creation, "one day" was thus an "evening then morning" or "darkness then dawning" day. Having defined the archetypal Creation day, the author thereafter referred back to that definition by means of ordinal numerals: "a second day"—that is, a second and similar day—"a third day," "a fourth day" (1:8, 13, 19). This is the way we still use our own language when we have carefully defined something and want to refer to additional instances of the same kind.

The narrative context for the designation of the archetypical Creation day is worth examining. Light had just been created and it was good (*tob*)—that is, it functioned as God intended[3]— implying that the precreation darkness did *not* fulfill God's purpose. The fully functional light was named "day" (*yom*) in contrast to the less-than-satisfactory darkness, which was named "night." Here "day" clearly referred to the "daytime" in which work was accomplished. In the next sentence, however, the author expands the word *day* (*yom*) to include not just the "dawning" of daylight (*boqer*) but also the preceding darkness of evening (*'ereb*).

What meaning did the hearers get from this expanded meaning of the word *day*? That this "day" was different from the immediately preceding "day" is clear. It begins, not with the arrival of light but with a word meaning dusk, twilight, or evening—that which is associated with the futile darkness.[4] Defined by its inclusion of *evening* (*'ereb*) as well as *dawning* (*boqer*), it involved two elements—one preliminary, incomplete, unfulfilled, and unsatisfactory; the other actualized, complete, and fulfilled.

So the "Creation day" could not have been simply daylight, because it included *evening* as well as *dawning*. Nor could it have

---

3. Recall the discussion of the word *tob* and our translation of it as "functioned well" in chapter 2, including footnotes 22, 23.

4. Recall the discussion of the word *yom* and "[Creation] day" in chapter 2.

meant an indefinite period of time or functioned as a general reference to time, because it was specifically defined by the preliminary *evening* and the subsequent *dawning*.

What is clear, however, is that the Creation days were times of God's extraordinary action—times during which momentous events took place, bringing into existence reality that did not previously exist, reality that was absolutely new. A Creation day was a time made significant by the transcendent activity of God.

FROM "EVENING" TO "DAWNING"

"There was evening, then dawning, one day" (Gen. 1:5). So what was the "day" made significant by God's creative activity that commenced with *evening* (*'ereb*) and concluded as *dawning* (*boqer*)?

The darkness with which the explanation of Creation opens is associated with pre-Creation formlessness and futility. We know this because its replacement, light, is described as *good*—that is, as useful, functioning as God intended (Gen. 1:4). The Hebrew *'ereb* connotes dusk and twilight (a mixture of light and dark). Its introduction in the Creation narrative recalls the preceding reference to the all-pervasive pre-Creation darkness, which God limited on the first Creation day by bringing light into existence. The direct referent for the *evening*-and-*dawning* day was what had just happened; at this point in the Creation narrative it was the only thing that had happened. Darkness, dusk, evening (*'ereb*) had become brightness, light, dawning (*boqer*).

In our consideration of the range of meanings of the word *day* (*yom*) it is useful to consider possible reasons for the author's unusual way of referring to each of the Creation days. Why was he at pains to specify that each of the first six days was an *evening*-then-*dawn*-

ing day? Why did he not describe the seventh day similarly? For us, it is dawning that begins a new day. It was so for the Hebrews as well, because the *day* was ordinarily a workday, a time of daylight, when something meaningful could be accomplished.

This is reflected in a series of stories confirming the fact that, for the Hebrews, the day began in the morning at least down to the time of the monarchy. Illustrating this usage, the narrator speaks of "tomorrow" in the context of "evening" or "night," indicating that the following morning—the "tomorrow"—marked the beginning of a new day. There are several such stories[5] in the Bible. The first is that of the incestuous relationship of Lot's daughters with their father: "They made their father drink wine that night. . . . The next day the firstborn said to the younger, 'Look, I lay last night with my father' " (Gen. 19:33, 34).

The next incident—also somewhat distressing—is that of a Levite and his concubine in the period of the Judges. "When the man with his concubine and his servant got up to leave, his father-in-law, the girl's father, said to him, 'Look, the day has worn on until it is almost evening. Spend the night. See, the day has drawn to a close. Spend the night here and enjoy yourself. Tomorrow you can get up early in the morning for your journey and go home' " (Judg. 19:9).

Several centuries later, David's wife Michal, the daughter of King Saul, warned her soon-to-be-king husband that Saul had sent messengers to his house to kill him the following morning. " 'If you do not save your life tonight, tomorrow you will be killed' " (1 Sam. 19:11).

---

5. Jacob Milgrom, *Leviticus 23–27*, vol. 3B, The Anchor Bible Commentaries (New York: Doubleday, 2001), 1967 cites these and other stories as indicating that the day for the Hebrews began in the morning. His Biblical references are Gen. 1:5; 19:33, 34; Lev. 7:15; 22:30; Num. 9:11; 33:3; Josh. 5:10; Judg. 19:4–9; 1 Sam. 19:11; 28:18, 19.

But if the day was understood to begin in the morning for the Hebrews down to the time of David, why did the author of Genesis 1 depart from the usual understanding and describe the Creation days as beginning with evening and proceeding to dawning? We will explore a possible answer to this question shortly.

For the present, however, since the author expanded the usual understanding of *day* (consisting of the daylight, warm, working hours) and the usual sequence of day followed by night, it would seem helpful to draw attention to this unusual usage when the text is translated into English. It is for this reason that we have translated the conjunction between *evening* and *dawning*" (Gen. 1:5) not as *and* but as *then*. The Hebrew word here (*w*) serves as a general, almost-all-purpose conjunction with English equivalents ranging through "and," "so," "then," "but," "now," and occasionally nothing at all. If, in fact, the author was describing the first Creation day as a reprise of the first creative act—the transformation from darkness to light—then one way to capture that sense in English (without being explicit, as the author wasn't) is to translate the Hebrew as "There was evening, then dawning—one [Creation] day" (Gen. 1:5b).

For later Hebrews the word *'ereb* often carried negative connotations.[6] The night that followed evening was a time of peril. "In the evening, sudden terror!" (Is. 17:14, NIV), and often a time of death.[7] It was a time when those who plotted evil would "come back, howling like dogs and prowling about the city" (Ps. 59:6, 14). By contrast, throughout the Hebrew Bible the word *boqer* carried no such negative freight. It meant

6. See H. Niehr, " *'ereb,*" in *Theological Dictionary of the Old Testament,* vol. 11, ed. G. Johannes Botterweck, Helmer Ringgren, and Heinz-Josef Fabry, trans. David E. Green (Grand Rapids, MI: Eerdmans, 2001), 340.
7. See 1 Kings 22:35; 2 Chron. 18:34; Ezek. 24:18; Ps. 90:6.

light, dawn, daybreak, sunrise, the end of fear and terror. Thus a *day* consisting of *evening* turned into *dawning* was good news indeed: a change of state, a transformation from darkness, threat, and menace to light, fulfillment, and satisfaction. "God saw that the light was good" (Gen. 1:4)—that is, it was fulfilling its divine purpose.

Having defined the archetypal Creation day and underscored its essential nature as a change of state from darkness to light, the author proceeded with an explanation of what was accomplished during the following Creation days. In each case, after describing God's creative activity he recapped the day as a transformation of some aspect of reality from a state of incompleteness (symbolized by *evening*) to a state of fulfillment (symbolized by *dawning*), moving step by step from formlessness and futility to form, functionality, and fulfillment of the divine purpose. In so doing God moved from "light mixed with darkness" to "darkness transformed into light." Here in Genesis 1 this is what Creation is, and a "Creation day" is a part of the process.

Evening and *dawning* have sometimes been understood metaphorically, with a part standing in for the whole (synecdoche). Thus *evening* meant night and *dawning* meant day. On this basis some readers have supposed that each of the Creation days was understood by the original hearers of Genesis 1 not as days in the realm of the divine, but rather as six modern twenty-four-hour, consecutive, solar days.

But as we have explained, this interpretation seems highly unlikely. If this was the picture the author wanted to convey, he could easily have combined the "day" and the "night" of the preceding sentence ("God named the light *day* and the darkness *night*) and designated the combined *day*-and-*night* sequence a "day." But he did not do that. Alternatively, he could have done something similar to what was done later in relation to the annual Day of Atonement (*Yom Kippur*): "From evening to evening you shall keep your sabbath" (Lev. 23:32). But he did not do that either.[8]

Yet it is undeniable that both the author of Genesis 1 and his listeners were aware of the period of time we call a twenty-four-hour solar day. It is clear from the entire thrust of this Creation account that the author intended these days of transcendent divine activity to be viewed as exemplars of human weekdays. This connection is explicit in the fourth commandment (Ex. 20:8–11) and a subsequent reiteration of the Sabbath law (31:12–17);[9] and it was certainly understood by the first listeners.

The six Creation days served as prologue to the Creator's Sabbath rest. Similarly six days in human life were to serve as a prologue to the Sabbath, the paradigmatic Biblical instance of *imitatio Dei* that established the week. That is why the author of Genesis 1 said, "God blessed the seventh day and made it sacred" (Gen. 2:3). The Sabbath rest was to be for humankind what the prototypical Sabbath rest was for God—a day of reflection on and celebration of God's acts of Creation.

---

8. This evening-to-evening designation is never applied to the weekly Sabbath in the Hebrew Bible, and the New Testament evidence is ambiguous. Later Jews, including observant Jews at the present time, have applied the *Yom Kippur* command in this way, as have Seventh-day Adventists.

9. This is the last explicit Scriptural connection of the Sabbath to Creation. Seventh-day Adventist readers and writers have often seen a connection in the First Angel's Message in Rev. 14. See, for example, John T. Baldwin, "Revelation 14:7: An Angel's Worldview," in *Creation, Catastrophe, and Calvary: Why a Global Flood Is Vital to the Doctrine of Atonement*, ed. John Templeton Baldwin (Hagerstown: Review and Herald, 2000), 19–39.

THE NUMBER SIX

The number six was used by the author for the sequence of Creation days and also for something else during the Creation week. In addition to the six days, there were six affirmations that aspects of Creation were "good" (*tob*)—in the sense of functioning well in the ways God intended they should (although the six affirmations do not correspond exactly to the six Creation days). As we noted in chapter 2, the Hebrew word *tob* can properly be translated as "functioning well" and thus fulfilling its purpose, communicating the truth that each aspect of created reality was "functionally good" in the utilitarian sense that other aspects of reality could then be based upon it or related to it. Six times, beginning with the creation of light, the author underscored the truth that God, in Creation, moved through a period of activities, in each case producing that which fulfilled God's purpose for that particular kind of reality:

- The first Creation day: God said, "Let there be light"; and God saw that it functioned well (1:4).
- The third day: God said, "Let the waters be gathered together, and let the dry land appear"; and God saw that they were functioning well (1:10).
- Also the third day: God said, "Let the earth bring forth seed-bearing plants and trees with seed-bearing fruit"; and God saw that they were functioning well (1:12).
- The fourth day: God said, "Let there be lights in the vault of the sky"; and God saw that they were functioning well (1:18).
- The fifth day: God said, "Let the water bring forth swarms of living creatures" and "let birds fly across the vault of the sky"; and God saw that they were functioning well (1:21).

- The sixth day: God said, "Let the earth bring forth creatures of every kind"; and God saw that they were functioning well (1:25).
- Finally God said, "Let us make the humankind in our image"; God saw that everything created functioned *very well* indeed (1:31).

Perhaps our focus on the six Creation days has been one-sided; perhaps we should have been just as interested in *how* the creative events of each day fulfilled God's intentions, culminating in the sixth day when what occurred was more than "satisfactory"; it fulfilled God's purpose *very well*. But the original listeners heard the *explanation*, not its *interpretation*. We too must first *hear* the explanation for what it is before proceeding to the interpretation. That is a further, theological task.

RECAPITULATION

To recap: each of the six days saw creative events that accomplished what they were intended to do.

- Light and its separation from darkness
- Dry land and its separation from sea
- Vegetation and its ordering into various "kinds"
- Lights in the heavens and their assignment as time-keepers
- Fish and fowl and their ordering into "kinds"
- Wild and domestic animals and their ordering into "kinds," plus male and female human beings and their appointment as stewards of the land.

All six evening-then-dawning Creation days were characterized by ordering and arranging by the Creator, moving created
reality toward its intended functionality. The Creation days thus
become archetypes—paradigms—of human weekdays. During
the week we, like God, are to bring—relatively, of course—light
from darkness and order from chaos. As creatures in the presence
and service of our Creator, we are called to use our time, energy,
and creativity to bring light and order as our talents allow.

SABBATH, CULMINATION OF THE SIX DAYS

The seventh day, at the end of Creation week, was the capstone of divine creative activity. On each of the six preceding
days in the realm of the divine, God had transformed a portion
of finite reality from a state of darkness, symbolized by evening
(*'ereb*) into a state of light, symbolized by dawning (*boqer*).
Because it was explicitly not a transformation of that which was
dark, disordered, and functionless into light, order, and function,
the seventh day is the first Creation *yom* not to be described by
evening and *dawning*. It was not just more of the same: on the
seventh day God rested.

As our human weekdays are given us so that we can, in our
own spheres of influence, work as the Creator worked "in the
beginning," so too we are given a seventh day for rest. This is
not, as often supposed, for us to "rest up" in order to work all
the more diligently and effectively during the next six days; it is
for us to experience in gratitude the satisfaction of accomplish-
ment. The seventh day is not for the sake of the six days; rather,
the six days are for the sake of the seventh. The Sabbath is "not
an interlude but the climax of living."[10]

---

10. Abraham Joshua Heschel, *The Sabbath: Its Meaning for Modern Man*, 14.

By failing to remember that the six Creation days were a divine prologue to that first Sabbath, we run the risk of missing the purpose for which we are granted the privilege of "working while it is day" (see John 9:4). We are called to work six days a week to bring order out of chaos, and on the seventh to join the Creator in celebrating worthwhile tasks accomplished.

And what, one may well ask, is a "worthwhile task"? That too is part of the message of Genesis 1. A worthwhile task takes something disordered, chaotic, dark, formless, and unproductive, and renders it ordered, organized, light, formed, and functional. In the author's words, a worthwhile task takes a state of *'ereb* and transforms it into a state of *boqer*. And the purpose of the seventh day is to allow us, in the presence of our Creator, to share in the joy of a worthwhile job well done.

Our work—our whole existence—is worthwhile to the extent that it transforms "there was evening" in our little section of the world into "then dawning."

WHAT GENESIS 1 REALLY SAYS

As the previous ten chapters have emphasized, before we address the question of what Genesis *says*, we have to consider what Genesis *said* to its original audience. Any recognition of what it says now is necessarily dependant on what it said then.

ABOUT LITERAL OR FIGURATIVE LANGUAGE

So we must ask, did that first Hebrew audience hear it as literal or as figurative? It has been the thesis of this book that the original Hebrew audience understood Genesis as a literal account of the coming-to-be of the "sky and the land and all that they contained." Those hearers did not need to make a choice between literal and figurative. It is those of us who read Genesis in the modern scientific era who wrestle with that problem.

It is, indeed, a momentous choice. Most of Christendom has opted for a *figurative* reading. But this choice raises another, equally challenging question: How many other literal-sounding Bible passages are to be understood figuratively? It is, however, similarly problematic to read Genesis as a *literal* description of the coming-to-be of our planet Earth and its life forms, the solar system of which Earth is a part, the Milky Way galaxy, and the vast universe beyond. On those matters the sciences (the archeological, earth, and astronomical sciences in particular) have much to say; and they do not now, and have not for several hundred years, come close to supporting a literal reading of Genesis 1—the efforts of Creationists notwithstanding.[1] Furthermore, for those who read Genesis literally in the twenty-first century, and who therefore regard the relevant scientific disciplines as erroneous, there is also a secondary question of enormous importance: If, in the light of Genesis, so much of modern science is in error, what remaining part of the scientific enterprise, if any, is to be trusted?

Not surprisingly, in reading the three-thousand-year-old text of Genesis 1 in the twenty-first century it is difficult for us to hear now what they heard then.

ABOUT THE HISTORY OF LIFE ON EARTH

Is it "evolution" or "Genesis"? As with most philosophical and many theological questions, the answer to this one is, "It all depends." In this case the answer depends on what we mean by "evolution."

We can readily distinguish three meanings of the word *evolution*—that is, three principal ways in which the word is used in conversations about creation and evolution. These are, of course, in addition to the many more general uses of *evolution* to refer to various kinds of development—as in references to

---

1. See, for example, L. James Gibson and Humberto M. Rasi, eds., *Understanding Creation, Answers to Questions on Faith and Science* (Nampa, ID: Pacific Press, 2011).

AFTERWORD ❧ 163

"the evolution of the modern idea of democracy," or "the evolution of women's clothing."

We can identify these three meanings as "Evolution$_1$" (E_1), "Evolution$_2$" (E_2), and "Evolution$_3$" (E_3). They are obviously related, and their relationships are the reason why they are so often confused with one another, even by scientists and theologians who should know better. They are also significantly different, and their differences are the reason why it is so important to distinguish among them. Failure to do so has resulted not only in unfortunate failure to communicate, but also in unnecessary damage to personal relationships and professional reputations.

- E_1 is the idea of long periods of time and major changes in the known forms of life on Earth. This idea involves "descent with modification," but does not specify the means by which the modification occurs.
- E_2 includes "Evolution$_1$" and adds the ideas of random genetic mutation and natural selection as means of major changes in life forms.
- E_3 includes both "Evolution$_1$" and "Evolution$_2$," and adds the twofold idea that "Evolution$_2$" provides a complete explanation for the existence of all known reality and the occurrence of all known phenomena, and that therefore there is no reality corresponding to the word "God" (or "Yahweh" or "Allah").

Our first observation is that E_1 and E_2 are scientific ideas, but that E_3 is a *non*scientific, philosophical idea. This does not make E_3 any more or less important than the other two, but it does mean that it is a different *kind* of idea and cannot be properly derived (factually or logically) from the others.

Our second observation is that Genesis 1 says nothing about

the accuracy or adequacy of the scientific ideas E_1 or E_2. These ideas must be confirmed or disconfirmed by relevant scientific evidence. If either E_1 or E_2 is what we mean by "evolution," then the answer to our question, "Does Genesis 1 say anything about evolution?" is clearly No.

On the other hand, E_3 is a philosophical idea that is logically incompatible with, and explicitly denied by, Genesis 1. So if (and only if) E_3 or something very much like it is what we mean by "evolution," then the answer to our question is emphatically Yes, because Genesis is a religious and theological rejection of E_3. In this broad sense, creationism is entailed by belief in God, YAHWEH, or Allah. This vigorous rejection of E_3 does not in itself disprove it; that issue must, and can readily, be argued on other grounds. At the same time, we note that while E_3 rejects the reality of God, it no more disproves that reality than it disproves the reality of interpersonal love or moral virtue (sociobiology[2] to the contrary not withstanding).

ABOUT GOD

If Genesis 1 doesn't say "that which is correct" about science—as we presently understand science—can it say "that which is correct" about God?

This question underscores one of the greatest hazards of placing scientific demands on an ancient text whose author had no such thing in mind. Implicit in this query is the assumption that theological truth and scientific truth use language in the same way. But the fact is that they don't. As many contemporary

---

2. See, for example, E. O. Wilson, *Sociobiology* (Cambridge, MA: Harvard, 1975, 2000), and *Consilience: The Unity of Knowledge* (New York: Vintage, 1999).

philosophers would say, theology and science are different "language games."[3]

A little reflection shows that this is correct. Throughout the Bible, God is described in human language, using human analogies; how else *could* the Ultimate, Transcendent, and Ineffable be described? This is as true for us as it was for the ancient Hebrews. For them, God was the Owner of the cattle on a thousand hills (Ps. 50:10). God was "LORD of hosts" (1 Sam. 1:11)—that is, more literally, "YAHWEH of retinues." This latter designation meant that God had larger armies available than did any kings—though this meaning has been updated and at the same time watered down in some recent versions as "LORD Almighty" (NIV, TNIV) and "LORD All-Powerful" (CEV). As human beings we can contemplate Deity only by analogy to what we experience in our human existence.

"What we experience" now includes an awareness of ten sextillion suns (chapter 7). When Job heard that God's throne was higher than the highest stars (Job 22:12) and Abraham heard that he should go out under the night sky and count the stars (Gen. 15:5), exactly how many stars could Abraham have counted? (We assume that Job was in no better position to argue with God about their height than to know how many billion light-years away they were.) The answer to the question about the number of stars the unaided eye can see is a little "soft" because it depends on the amount of light pollution where the count is done and the sensitivity of the retina of the one doing the counting. Allowing for those uncertainties, the number is no more than about six thousand.

So the God of the first listeners to Genesis 1 was known as

---

3. The helpful idea of "language games" was introduced by Ludwig Wittgenstein, *Philosophical Investigations*, trans. G. E. M. Anscombe (Englewood Cliffs, NJ: Prentice Hall, 1973).

the One who created the sun, moon, and six thousand stars to light up the earth. Thanks to the Hubble telescope, the God of the twenty-first-century listeners to Genesis 1 is known as the One who created ten sextillion suns (with some smaller and some much larger). Does this mean that our God is seventeen-hundred quadrillion times greater than theirs was? The question itself is absurd, because the "greatness" of God is not a matter of arithmetic, even if our still-very-limited understanding of God's "greatness" seems in some sense to have enlarged along with our scientific conception of the size and contents of the universe.[4]

Are we any closer to appreciating God's infinity now than they were then? The answer is, "Perhaps, but not really." The creation of ten sextillion suns over 13.7 billion years versus the placement of six thousand points of light in "the vault of the sky" certainly indicates that the spatial extent of known reality is unimaginably greater, so that in that sense the scope of God's creative activity is known to be larger. But if we think of space as unbounded, created reality as unimaginably large, and God as infinite, then in an important sense the difference between the ancients' conception of God and ours is hardly significant.

But that, as we sometimes say, "isn't the half of it." With all our progress at enlarging the scope and scale of the known universe we have—for the moment—reached an interesting point. For the first time in the history of space exploration we are reasonably sure that everything we can detect with our best telescopes—everything whose light we can analyze—makes up only about 4 percent of what is out there. Dark matter and dark energy are at present (and for good and proper scientific reasons) thought to constitute more than 96 percent of the mass of which

---

4. The current cosmological speculation about the possibility of parallel universes that constitute a "multiverse" is not relevant to our present concern.

the universe is made. Of all people at all times and in all places, we should be the wariest of claiming that our knowledge of science is a surety; that our resulting knowledge of God as reflected in the physical results of Creation is "correct."

Furthermore, God's "greatness" is not finally measured in cosmological terms, even if our growing knowledge of the cosmos is (as we hope) actually characterized by "increasing verisimilitude."[5] So we can properly say that in the most important sense, the "God knowledge" of the original hearers of Genesis 1 was not wrong but *right*—right in the sense that it was knowledge about what is ultimately important, and right also in the sense that what they understood is ultimately *true*. For to know about the cosmos—for example, when and how it came into existence—is at most interesting; but to know that our universe, including ourselves, is the result of the gracious activity of an infinitely loving God—that makes all the difference for the meaning of our lives and for the way we live. Clearly—and happily—the correctness of our scientific knowledge about God's Creation is not a prerequisite for the "truth" of our comprehension of God.

Scripture is first and foremost about God and God's relation to human beings; it is only secondarily about physical reality and its constituent parts such as "sky," "land," and "sea." The explanatory categories (what we called "explanacepts" in chapter 6) have changed radically for physical reality, which was transferred from the realm of "God" to "nature" and "chance." As a result, what we hear about physical reality now is very different from

---

5. This phrase is used by John Polkinghorne to characterize modern science. See *Beyond Science: The Wider Human Context* (New York: Cambridge, 1996), 8, and *Faith, Science and Understanding* (New Haven, CT: Yale, 2000), 79: "Scientists are mapmakers of the physical world. . . . In the sense of an increasing verisimilitude, of ever better approximations to the truth of the matter, science offers us a tightening grasp of physical reality."

what the first Hebrew listeners heard in Genesis 1. That is emphatically not the case for Biblical affirmations about God, which are the primary reason why Scripture exists. Statements about God and the relationship of God to human beings, then as now, are located in the explanatory concept "God." True, our understanding of God has been enlarged and filled out through the centuries, but the basic explanatory concept has remained constant. The path to God is constant, and the life-altering function of Scripture in leading the searcher-for-truth down that path has remained the same for three thousand years.

So, while we know much more about God's physical universe than did the original hearers of Genesis 1, through God's self-revelation in the life, death, and resurrection of Jesus of Nazareth, we have also learned much more about what God is, what God does, and what God wants. But that is the subject for another, very different, and ultimately more important book.

BIBLIOGRAPHY

Alter, Robert. *Genesis: Translation and Commentary.* New York:
Norton, 1996.

Augustine, Saint. *The Literal Meaning of Genesis.* Translated by John
Hammond Taylor. 2 vols. Ancient Christian Writers 41, 42.
Westminster, MD: Newman, 1982.

Baldwin, John Templeton, ed. *Creation, Catastrophe, and Calvary:
Why a Global Flood Is Vital to the Doctrine of Atonement.*
Hagerstown, MD: Review and Herald, 2000.

Bauckham, Richard. *The Bible and Ecology: Rediscovering the
Community of Creation.* Sarum Theological Lectures. Waco,
TX: Baylor, 2010.

Bede. *Bede: On Genesis.* Translated by Calvin B. Kendall. Translated
Texts for Historians. Liverpool, UK: Liverpool University
Press, 2008.

Beaude, Pierre-Marie. *The Book of Creation.* Translated by Andrew
Clements. Illustrated by Georges Lemoine. Saxonville, MA:
Picture Book Studio, 1991.

Bergman, Jan, and Magnus Ottosson. "'erets." In *Theological
Dictionary of the Old Testament,* vol. 1. Edited by G. Johannes
Botterweck and Helmer Ringgren. Translated by John T.
Willis. Grand Rapids, MI: Eerdmans, 1974.

Berry, R. J. "I Believe in God, Maker of Heaven and Earth." In
Real Scientists, Real Faith, 5–12. Edited by R. J. Berry. Grand
Rapids, MI: Monarch, 2009.

Blocher, Henri. *In the Beginning: The Opening Chapters of Genesis.*
Translated by David G. Preston. Downers Grove, IL:
InterVarsity, 1984.

Boice, James Montgomery. *Genesis: An Expositional Commentary.* 3
vols. Grand Rapids, MI: Zondervan, 1982, 1985, 1987.

Brueggemann, Walter. *Genesis.* Interpretation: A Bible Commentary for Teaching and Preaching. Atlanta: John Knox, 1982.

Burke, James. *The Day the Universe Changed.* Boston: Little, Brown, 1985.

Cassuto, Umberto. *A Commentary on the Book of Genesis, Part I: From Adam to Noah.* Translated by Israel Abrahams. Jerusalem: Magnes/Hebrew University, 1961.

Collins, C. John. *Genesis 1–4: A Linguistic, Literary, and Theological Commentary.* Phillipsburg, NJ: P & R, 2006.

Cotter, David W. *Genesis.* Berit Olam Studies in Hebrew Narrative & Poetry. Collegeville, MN: Liturgical Press, 2003.

Documents from Old Testament Times. Translated by members of the Society for Old Testament Study. Edited by D. Winton Thomas. New York: Harper & Row, 1961.

Doukhan, Jacques. "The Literary Structure of the Genesis Creation Story." Th.D. diss., Andrews University, 1978.

Eichrodt, Walter. "In the Beginning: A Contribution to the Interpretation of the First Word of the Bible." In *Creation in the Old Testament,* 65–73. Edited by Bernhard W. Anderson. Philadelphia: Fortress, 1984.

Falk, Marcia. "Translation as a Journey." In *The Song of Songs: A New Translation and Interpretation,* 91–98. San Francisco: HarperSanFrancisco, 1990.

Fretheim, Terence E. *Creation, Fall, and Flood: Studies in Genesis 1-11.* Minneapolis: Augsburg, 1969.

———. "Genesis 1:1-2:3, The Creation." In *The New Interpreter's Bible: A Commentary in Twelve Volumes,* 1:338–47. Nashville: Abingdon, 1994.

Gibson, John C. L. *Genesis, Volume 1.* The Daily Study Bible: Old Testament. Louisville, KY: Westminster John Knox, 1981.

Gibson, L. James, and Humberto M. Rasi, eds. *Understanding Creation: Answers to Questions on Faith and Science.* Nampa, ID: Pacific Press, 2011.

Gilkey, Langdon B. *Maker of Heaven and Earth: A Study of the Christian Doctrine of Creation.* New York: Doubleday/Anchor, 1959.

Glover, Gordon J. *Beyond the Firmament: Understanding Science and the Theology of Creation.* Chesapeake, VA: Watertree, 2007.

Görg, M. "*raqiaʿ.*" *Theological Dictionary of the Old Testament* 13, 646–53. Edited by G. Johannes Botterweck, Helmer Ringgren, and Heinz-Josef Fabry. Translated by David E. Green. Grand Rapids, MI: Eerdmans, 2004.

Harper's Dictionary of the Bible. Edited by Paul J. Achtemeier. San Francisco: Harper and Row, 1985.

Heidel, Alexander. *The Babylonian Genesis: The Story of Creation.* 2nd ed. Chicago: University of Chicago Press, 1951.

Heschel, Abraham Joshua. *The Sabbath: Its Meaning for Modern Man.* New York: Farrar, Straus, 1959.

Hodge, B. C. *Revisiting the Days of Genesis: A Study of the Use of Time in Genesis 1–11 in Light of Its Ancient Near Eastern and Literary Context.* Eugene, OR: Wipf & Stock, 2011.

Horn, Siegfried H. "Firmament." *Seventh-day Adventist Bible Dictionary,* Commentary Reference Series, 8. Washington, DC: Review and Herald, 1960.

Höver-Johag, I. "*tob.*" In *Theological Dictionary of the Old Testament* 5, 296–317. Edited by G. Johannes Botterweck and Helmer Ringgren. Translated by David E. Green. Grand Rapids, MI: Eerdmans, 1986.

Jacob, Benno. *The First Book of the Bible: Genesis.* Edited and translated by Ernest I. Jacob and Walter Jacob. Jersey City, NJ: Ktav, 1974.

Jaki, Stanley L. *Genesis 1 Through the Ages.* London: Thomas More, 1992.

Kass, Leon. *The Beginning of Wisdom: Reading Genesis.* New York: Free Press, 2003.

Koehler, Ludwig, and Walter Baumbartner, eds. *Lexicon in Veteris Testamenti Libros.* Grand Rapids, MI: Eerdmans, 1958.

Lamoureux, Denis O. *Evolutionary Creation: A Christian Approach to Evolution.* Eugene, OR: Wipf and Stock, 2008.

Langford, Jerome P. *Galileo, Science and the Church.* 3rd ed. Ann Arbor: University of Michigan Press, 1992.

Long, Charles H. *Alpha: The Myths of Creation.* Classics in Religious
    Studies 4. Chico, CA: Scholars Press, 1963.
Luther, Martin. *Luther's Commentary on Genesis.* 2 vols. Translated
    by J. Theodore Mueller. Grand Rapids, MI: Zondervan, 1958.
Mathews, Kenneth A. *Genesis 1–11:26.* Vol. 1a of *New American
    Commentary: An Exegetical and Theological Exposition of Holy
    Scripture.* Nashville: Broadman and Holman, 1996.
Milgrom, Jacob. *Leviticus 23–27.* The Anchor Bible Commentaries
    3B. New York: Doubleday, 2001.
Mitchell, Stephen. *Genesis: A New Translation of the Classic Biblical
    Stories.* New York: HarperCollins, 1996.
Moltmann, Jürgen. *God in Creation: A New Theology of Creation
    and the Spirit of God.* Translated by Margaret Kohl. San
    Francisco: Harper and Row, 1985.
Morris, Henry M. *The Genesis Record: A Scientific and Devotional
    Commentary on the Book of Beginnings.* Grand Rapids, MI:
    Baker, 1976.
Moyers, Bill D. *Genesis: A Living Conversation.* Edited by Betty Sue
    Flowers. New York, Doubleday, 1996.
Niehr, H. "'ereb." In *Theological Dictionary of the Old Testament* 11,
    335–41. Edited by G. Johannes Botterweck, Helmer Ringgren,
    and Heinz-Josef Fabry. Translated by David E. Green. Grand
    Rapids, MI: Eerdmans, 2001.
Numbers, Ronald L. *The Creationists: From Scientific Creationism
    to Intelligent Design.* Expanded ed. Cambridge, MA: Harvard,
    2006.
————. "Science Without God: Natural Law and Christian
    Beliefs." In *When Science and Christianity Meet,* 265–85.
    Edited by David C. Lindberg and Ronald L. Numbers.
    Chicago: University of Chicago Press, 2003.
————. ed. *Galileo Goes to Jail and Other Myths about Science and
    Religion.* Cambridge, MA: Harvard, 2009.
Polkinghorne, John. *Beyond Science: The Wider Human Context.* New
    York: Cambridge, 1996.
————. *Faith, Science and Understanding.* New Haven, CT: Yale, 2000.

————. *Scientists as Theologians: A Comparison of the Writings of Ian Barbour, Arthur Peacock, and John Polkinghorne.* London: SPCK, 1996.

Rad, Gerhard von. *Genesis: A Commentary.* Revised edition. Translated by John H. Marks. The Old Testament Library. Philadelphia: Westminster, 1972.

Ross, Allen P. *Creation and Blessing: A Guide to the Study and Exposition of Genesis.* Grand Rapids, MI: Baker, 1988.

Saebø, M. "*yom*, II-III." In *Theological Dictionary of the Old Testament* 6, 12–32. Edited by G. Johannes Botterweck and Helmer Ringgren. Translated by David E. Green. Grand Rapids, MI: Eerdmans, 1990.

Sailhamer, John H. *Genesis Unbound: A Provocative New Look at the Creation Account.* Sisters, OR: Multnomah, 1996.

Sarna, Nahum M. *Genesis.* The JPS Torah Commentary. Philadelphia: Jewish Publication Society, 1989.

————. *Understanding Genesis: The World of the Bible in the Light of History.* New York: Schocken, 1966.

SBL Handbook of Style: For Ancient Near Eastern, Biblical, and Early Christian Studies. Edited by Patrick H. Alexander et al. Peabody, MA: Hendrickson, 1999.

Seventh-day Adventist Bible Commentary, vol. 1. Edited by Francis D. Nichol et al. Washington: DC: Review and Herald, 1953.

Simpkins, Ronald A. "Worldview." In *Eerdmans Dictionary of the Bible.* Edited by David N. Freedman. Grand Rapids, MI: Eerdmans, 2000.

Soden, W. von, J. Bergman, and M. Saebø. "*yom.*" In *Theological Dictionary of the Old Testament* 6. Edited by G. Johannes Botterweck and Helmer Ringgren. Translated by David E. Green. Grand Rapids, MI: Eerdmans, 1990.

Speiser, E. A. *Genesis.* The Anchor Bible Commentaries 1. Garden City, NY: Doubleday, 1964.

Stek, John H. "What Says the Scripture?" In *Portraits of Creation: Biblical and Scientific Perspectives on the World's Formation,* 203–65. Edited by Howard J. Van Till. Grand Rapids, MI: Eerdmans, 1990.

Straus, Leo. "On the Interpretation of Genesis" [1957]. In Leo
    Strauss, *Jewish Philosophy and the Crisis of Modernity: Essays and
    Lectures in Modern Jewish Thought.* 359–76. Edited by Kenneth
    Hart Green. Albany: State University of New York Press, 1997.
Tarnas, Richard. *The Passion of the Western Mind: Understanding the
    Ideas That Have Shaped Our World View.* New York: Ballantine,
    1991.
Tucker, W. Dennis, Jr. "Firmament." In *Eerdmans Dictionary of the
    Bible.* Edited by David N. Freedman et al. Grand Rapids, MI:
    Eerdmans, 2000.
Turner, Laurence A. *Genesis.* Readings: A New Biblical
    Commentary. Sheffield, U.K.: Sheffield Academic, 2000.
*Tyndale's Old Testament: Being the Pentateuch of 1530, Joshua to 2
    Chronicles of 1537, and Jonah.* Translated by William Tyndale.
    New Haven, CT: Yale, 1992.
Waltke, Bruce K., with Cathi J. Fredricks. *Genesis: A Commentary.*
    Grand Rapids, MI: Zondervan, 2001.
Walton, John H. *The Lost World of Genesis One: Ancient Cosmology
    and the Origins Debate.* Downers Grove, IL: InterVarsity, 2009.
Watts, J. Wash. *A Distinctive Translation of Genesis.* Grand Rapids,
    MI: Eerdmans, 1963.
Wenham, Gordon J. *Genesis 1–15.* Vol. 1 of Word Biblical
    Commentary. Waco, TX: Word, 1987.
Westermann, Claus. *Creation.* Translated by John J. Scullion.
    Philadelphia: Fortress, 1974.
———. *Genesis: A Practical Commentary, Text and Interpretation.*
    Translated by David E. Green. Grand Rapids, MI: Eerdmans,
    1987.
White, Ellen G. "Christ Our Hope." *Advent Review and Sabbath
    Herald,* Dec. 20, 1892, 785. Reprinted in *Counsels to Writers
    and Editors,* 35. Nashville: Southern Publishing Association,
    1946.
———. *Education.* Mountain View, CA: Pacific Press, 1903, 1942.
———. *The Story of Patriarchs and Prophets: The Conflict of the Ages
    Illustrated in the Lives of Holy Men of Old.* Mountain View,

CA: Pacific Press, 1890, 1913.

———. *Thoughts from the Mount of Blessing.* Mountain View, CA: Pacific Press, 1900, 1943.

Wilson, Edward O. *Consilience: The Unity of Knowledge.* New York: Alfred Knopf, 1998.

———. *Sociobiology: The New Synthesis.* Cambridge, MA: Harvard, 1975, 2000.

Wittgenstein, Ludwig. *Philosophical Investigations.* Translated by G. E. M. Anscombe. New York: Prentice Hall, 1973.

Wright, J. Edward. "Cosmogony, Cosmology." In *The New Interpreter's Dictionary of the Bible,* vol. 1. Edited by Katharine Doob Sakenfeld. Nashville: Abingdon, 2006.

Young, Edward J. *Studies in Genesis One.* International Library of Philosophy and Theology: Biblical and Theological Studies. Philadelphia: P & R, 1999.

INDEX

defined, 21–22
imperfections of, 24–25
spectrum of goals in, 21
translations, Biblical
conservative tendencies of, 25–26
in English
chronological list, 31–33
translations, modern English
"verbal inspiration" re, 81–85
translation *vs.* paraphrase, 135, 136
transmission, textual, 80–84
and Holy Spirit, 80
Tropic of Cancer, 117
truth
close investigation &, xii–xiii
tsabaoth
translated, 45
tsunami
as "act of God," 95–96
Tucker, W. Dennis, Jr., 41n
Turner, Laurence A., 46n
twenty-first century
four explanacepts of, 98–99
limited knowledge in, 90
two Creations explanation
unlikeliness of, 137–138
two-explanacept world
of Genesis 1, 103–104
Tyche, 102
Tyndale House, Cambridge, xiii
Tyndale's Old Testament (TOT), 31
Tyndale, William, 31
selects translation "heaven," 56

U

unexplainable, the
explaining of, 95–107
universe
expanding, 93
irrelevance of idea to Genesis, 34–35
modern conceptions of, 111–113
vs. "the sky and the land," 109–119
universe
defined, 115–116
universe & Genesis 1
unexamined assumptions re, 109–111
universe, post-Hubble, 57

V

value
scientism's conception of, 105

vast array
term explained, 45
vault, 24, 106
ancient concept of, 49–62
disappearance of, 69–71, 74
in Ezekiel's vision, 72
functions of, 71–72, 125
ignominious fate of, 70
importance of, 67–68, 69–70, 71–77
objections to, 71
to prophet and community, 88
as protecting all Creation, 76–77
in Psalm 19:1, 71
purpose of, 68
re Creation days 1–3, 66
as stable environment, 125
as subject of Genesis 1, 67–68
word choice explained, 34–35, 40–41
vault, 60–62
connotations of word, 61–62
times named in Genesis 1, 67–68
vault and sky
pairing of, 66
vault of the sky
importance of, 65
phrase of transition, 66, 67–68
vault of the sky
contrasted with *universe*, 115–116
defined, 115
as realm of the gods, 114
term contrasted with *universe*, 115–119
vegetation and food
pairing of, 66
verbal inspiration, 80
verb tense, pluperfect
in harmonizing attempt, 52n
vocabulary, Genesis 1
defining words of, 24
Vulgate, 25, 60

W

Waltke, Bruce K., 47n
Walton, John H., 34, 53n
water
as chaos, as source of life, 53
pre-existence of, 123–124
prior to creation, 23, 24
waters
of chaos, 59–60
under the vault, 63n
water(s)